The Salton Sea: An Account Of Harriman's Fight With The Colorado River

George Kennan

In the interest of creating a more extensive selection of rare historical book reprints, we have chosen to reproduce this title even though it may possibly have occasional imperfections such as missing and blurred pages, missing text, poor pictures, markings, dark backgrounds and other reproduction issues beyond our control. Because this work is culturally important, we have made it available as a part of our commitment to protecting, preserving and promoting the world's literature. Thank you for your understanding.

THE SALTON SEA

AN ACCOUNT OF HARRIMAN'S FIGHT WITH THE COLORADO RIVER

BY
GEORGE KENNAN

ILLUSTRATED

New York
THE MACMILLAN COMPANY
1917

All rights reserved

COPYRIGHT, 1917
By THE MACMILLAN COMPANY
Set up and printed. Published May, 1917.

The Salton Sea in August 1906

Frontispiece

FOREWORD

I desire gratefully to acknowledge my indebtedness to the Smithsonian Institution, the U. S. Reclamation Service, the U. S. Geological Survey, the American Society of Civil Engineers, and the officials of the Southern Pacific Railroad Company, for their courtesy in furnishing me information, or permitting me to make use of their maps, diagrams and illustrations.

GEORGE KENNAN.

CONTENTS

	PAGES
1. THE SALTON SINK	5
2. THE CREATION OF THE OASIS	18
3. THE RUNAWAY RIVER	31
4. THE SAVING OF THE VALLEY	61
5. THE RECOMPENSE	93

ILLUSTRATIONS

The Salton Sea in August, 1906....*Frontispiece*

Opposite page

Relief Map of Imperial Valley	19
A Part of Colorado River Watershed	31
Agricultural Lands Eroded	57
A Flood Waterfall Nearer View of Flood Cataract	58
Channel Cut by Runaway River	60
Hind-Clarke Dam Railroad Track on Reconstructed Levee	89

THE SALTON SEA

THE SALTON SEA

> "The desert waited, silent, hot and fierce in its desolation, holding its treasures under the seal of death against the coming of the strong ones." (*Inscription over the main entrance to the Barbara Worth Hotel, El Centro, Imperial Valley.*)

No series of events in the history of southern California is more interesting, or more dramatic, than the creation of the beautiful and fertile oasis of the Imperial Valley in the arid desert-basin of the Salton Sink; the partial transformation of this cultivated valley into a great Inland Sea by the furious inpour of a runaway river; the barring out of the flood by the courage and energy of a single man, and the final development of the valley into one of the richest agricultural areas in the world.

Sixteen years ago, the region whose productiveness now rivals that of the lower Nile was the dried-up bottom of an ancient sea. It was seldom sprinkled by rain; it was scorched by sunshine of almost equatorial intensity, and during the summer months its mirage-haunted

THE SALTON SEA

air was frequently heated to a temperature of 120 degrees. The greater part of it lay far below the level of the sea; nearly all of it was destitute of water and vegetation; furious dust and sand storms swept across it, and it was regarded, by all the early explorers of the Southwest, as perhaps the dreariest and most forbidding desert on the North American continent. This ancient sea-basin, which thousands of years ago held the northern part of the Gulf of California, is now the Imperial Valley—a vast agricultural and horticultural hothouse, which produces almost everything that can be grown in lower Egypt, and which has recently been described in the San Francisco Argonaut as "potentially the richest unified district in the United States."

As recently as the year 1900, the Imperial Valley had not a single civilized inhabitant, and not one of its hot, arid acres had ever been cultivated. It now has a population of more than forty thousand, with churches, banks, ice factories, electric-light plants and fine school buildings, in half a dozen prosperous towns, and its 400,000 acres of cultivated land have produced, in the last six or eight years, crops to the value of at least $50,000,000. The history of this fertile oasis in the Colorado Desert will

THE SALTON SEA

forever be connected with the name of E. H. Harriman. He did not create the Imperial Valley, nor did he develop it; but he saved it from ruinous devastation at a time when the agency that had created it threatened capriciously to destroy it, and when there was no other power in the world that could give it protection.

THE SALTON SINK

The story of the Imperial Valley begins with the formation, in remote geologic times, of the great shallow depression, or basin, which modern explorers have called the Salton Sink. Tens of thousands of years ago, before the appearance of man on earth, the long arm of the Pacific Ocean which is now known as the Gulf of California extended in a northwesterly direction to a point more than a hundred miles distant from its present head. Its terminus was then near the San Gorgonio pass, about ninety miles east of the place where Los Angeles now stands, and it extended across the Colorado Desert to the site of the present town of Yuma. If it had not been affected by external forces, it would probably have retained to the present day its ancient boundary line; but into it, on

THE SALTON SEA

its eastern side, happened to empty one of the mightiest rivers of the Great West—the Colorado—and by this agency the upper part of the Gulf was gradually separated from the lower, and was finally turned into a salt-water lake, equal in extent to the Great Salt Lake in Utah. This detached body of ocean water, which had formerly been the upper part of the Gulf of California, completely filled the basin of the Salton Sink, and had an area of approximately 2100 square miles.

"But how," it may be asked, "could a river, however mighty, cut the Gulf of California in two, so as to separate the upper part from the lower and leave the former isolated?" Easily enough in the long ages of geologic time. A great river like the Colorado does not consist of water only. It holds in suspension and carries down to the sea a great load of sediment, which, when deposited at its mouth, gradually builds up a delta-plain of mud, and often changes topographical conditions over a wide area. It was this deposited sediment that cut the Gulf of California in two. The drainage basin of the Colorado and its tributaries extends from the Gulf of California to the southern edge of the Yellowstone National Park, and has an area of more than 260,000 square miles. Most of this area is mountainous, and the innumerable streams that tear down through its gorges and ravines erode and gather up vast quantities of sediment, which the river carries to the Gulf and finally deposits in its waters. How great a load of silt the Colorado brought down in prehistoric times we have no means of knowing; but it transports past Yuma now about 160,000,000 tons of solid matter every year, or enough to fill a reservoir one mile square to a depth of one hundred and twenty five feet.[1] Century after century, the river poured this vast quantity of silt into the Gulf opposite its mouth, and gradually built up a delta-bar which extended westward, year by year, until it finally reached the opposite coast. The upper part of the Gulf was then separated from the lower by a natural levee, in the shape of a delta-plain, which was perhaps ten miles in width by thirty in length, and which extended from a point near the present site of Yuma to the rampart of the Cocopah Mountains at Black Butte. When the river had thus cut the Gulf of California in two, it happened to choose a course for itself on the southeastern side of the delta-plain that it had built up, and thereafter it discharged its waters into the lower Gulf,

[1] Rep. of U. S. Geolog. Survey for 1916.

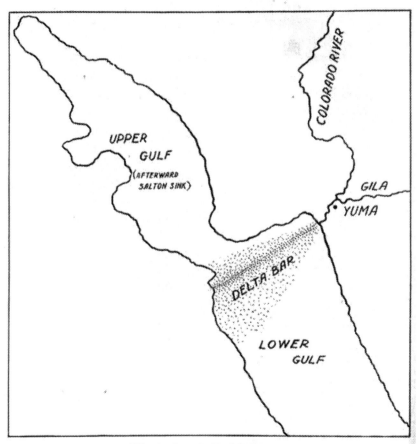

The Ancient Gulf of California

THE SALTON SEA

leaving what had been the upper Gulf isolated as a salt-water lake. Under the burning sun of that region about six feet of water evaporates every year, and in course of time the lake dried up, leaving the arid basin afterward known as the Salton Sink. This depression was about one hundred miles in length by thirty five in width. It then had a maximum depth of perhaps one thousand feet, and in the deeper parts its floor was covered with an incrustation of salt.

How long this ancient sea-bottom remained dry cannot now be determined; but many thousands of years ago, probably in Middle Tertiary times the Colorado River, which had first cut off the basin from the ocean and thus allowed it to become waterless, proceeded to refill it. Running over a raised delta-plain of silt, which sloped both ways, the river could easily be diverted to either side, and in one of its prehistoric floods it capriciously changed its course, leaving the Gulf and pouring its waters into the dry basin of the Salton Sink. When it had refilled this basin, and transformed it into a great fresh-water lake, it broke through the silt dam, or levee, on the Cocopah Mountain side, and found a new outlet to the Gulf through what is now known as Hardy's Colorado. For many years—possibly for centuries—the Salton

THE SALTON SEA

Sink was a fresh-water lake, into which the Colorado poured 150,000,000 tons or more of silt every year. At last, suddenly or gradually, the river again changed its course, abandoning the Sink and cutting a channel to the Gulf through the eastern part of the delta-plain. Then the Salton Sea again dried up, leaving a two-hundred-mile ellipse of fresh-water shells to mark its former level.

How many times, since the Tertiary epoch, the Salton Sink has been alternately emptied and refilled, we have no means of knowing; but the instability of the conditions that now determine the course of the Colorado below Yuma seem to indicate that, at intervals of four or five hundred years for many millenniums, the river, like a great liquid pendulum, swung back and forth across its delta, now emptying into the Gulf on the Arizona side, and then discharging into the Sink on the California side. Every time the lake was deprived of the river water it dried up, and every time the Sink was revisited by the river it again became a lake. That the Colorado must have returned to this basin many times, and flowed into it for long periods, is indicated by the fact that after the Sink was separated from the Gulf of California, the river carried into it something like seventeen cubic miles of silt.[1] Artesian well borings at Holtville show that the sedimentary deposits in that part of the Imperial Valley are now more than 1000 feet in depth.

For three centuries or more—from 1540 to 1902—the Salton Sink was a hot, arid desert. Melchior Diaz, a Spanish explorer in the service of Cortes, reached the edge of it in the fall of 1540, and the Spanish captain Juan Butista de Anza crossed it two hundred and thirty four years later; but neither of them saw anything like a lake. The only evidence that the Colorado River ran into the Sink, at any time between 1540 and 1905, is furnished by the so-called Rocque map, now in the British Museum, which was compiled from all the sources of information that were in existence in 1762. This map shows a considerable body of water in the Salton Sink, with the Colorado River flowing into it; but no written record in support of the map has ever been found, and the probability is that the water was nothing more than a comparatively small lake, or lagoon, fed

---

[1] "The Imperial Valley and Salton Sink," by H. T. Cory, formerly Chief Engineer of the California Development Co., p. 49; San Francisco 1915 (embodying paper read Jan. 8, 1913, before the Amer. Soc. of Civil Engineers and published in its Transactions as "Paper 1270").

THE SALTON SEA

by the Colorado in time of flood. Overflow water in considerable quantities often reached the basin when the river happened to be more than bank full; but the main current of the Colorado continued to flow into the Gulf, and the flood water in the Sink soon evaporated.

In the latter part of the 18th century and the first half of the 19th, many Spanish and American pathfinders crossed the Sink on their way from Yuma to the California missions, but none of them found anything like a lake. Colonel W. H. Emory, who traversed it with General Kearney in the fall of 1846, described it as a hot, arid desert, where there was a stretch of "ninety miles from water to water," and where no vegetation could be found except scattered desert shrubs and two small patches of sun-burned grass. Captain A. R. Johnson, who also accompanied the Kearney expedition, was the first to notice the fact that this stretch of waterless desert was the dried-up bottom of an ancient lake; but neither he nor Colonel Emory observed the still more suggestive fact that it was below the level of the sea. In the deepest part of the basin, near the present station of Salton, they discovered a small lagoon; but its water proved to be so saturated with alkali and salt that it was "wholly unfit for man or brute." Three years later, gold-seekers from the East began to take this route to the Pacific Coast, and Bayard Taylor, in his "Eldorado," has given their impressions of the Salton Sink in the following words:

"The emigrants by the Gila route gave a terrible account of the crossing of the Great Desert lying west of the Colorado. They described this region as scorching and sterile—a country of burning salt plains and shifting hills of sand, where the only signs of human habitation were the bones of animals and men scattered along the trails."

Such, seventy years ago, was the Salton Sink, and such it had been during the three preceding centuries of recorded history. If anyone had then ventured to predict that this dried-up bed of the Gulf of California, this hot, sterile and apparently irreclaimable desert, would eventually become a beautiful cultivated valley, producing cotton, barley, alfalfa, dates, melons and fruit, to the value of ten or fifteen million dollars every year, he would have been generally regarded as a visionary enthusiast, if not a desert-crazed monomaniac.

Although, at the beginning of the "gold rush" to California in 1849, the Salton Sink had been known to the Spaniards for more than

THE SALTON SEA

three centuries, and to American explorers for at least twenty years, no scientific examination of it had ever been made. Four years later, however, in 1853, Jefferson Davis, who was then Secretary of War, prevailed upon Congress to authorize a series of explorations for the discovery of a practicable railroad route to the Pacific Coast. Lieutenant R. S. Williamson, of the United States Topographic Engineers, was selected as leader of the southern expedition, and with him, as geologist, went Professor William P. Blake of New York, a young graduate of the Yale Scientific School, who afterward attained great distinction as geologist, explorer and mining engineer, in fields as widely separated as Arizona, Alaska and Japan. Professor Blake was the first to explain the origin of the Salton Sink, to trace its ancient history, and to give a name to the great fresh-water lake that it had once held. He was also the first to suggest the possibility of irrigating it, and to predict that when it should be supplied with water it would "yield crops of almost any kind." Reclamation of desert areas is now comparatively common; but sixty years ago, only a bold and original mind could have entertained the idea of getting crops out of such a "Death Valley" as the Salton Sink then was.

THE SALTON SEA

Professor Blake, however, had the imagination of an investigator, tempered by the accurate knowledge of a scientist, and he could see that the sedimentary deposits in that ancient sea-basin needed only water to make them fertile.

The Kearney expedition of 1846, and the Bartlett and Williamson surveys in 1850 and 1853, demonstrated the practicability of reaching California by the southern route, and thousands of emigrants, attracted to the Pacific Coast by the discovery of gold, went that way in order to avoid the high mountains and the snow that they would have encountered further north. This rising tide of travel soon led to improvement in the means of transportation. Early in the "gold rush," Dr. A. L. Lincoln, a relative of Abraham Lincoln, established a permanent ferry across the Colorado, near the junction of that river with the Gila; a few years later, seventy four camels and dromedaries were imported from Africa for use on the desert part of the route; and in 1857, a private company began running bimonthly stages between San Antonio, Texas, and San Diego, California. Finally, in 1858, the Government established the "Butterfield Overland Mail," which ran a semi-weekly line of coaches from St. Louis to San Francisco, by way of El

THE SALTON SEA

Paso, Yuma and the Colorado Desert, on a time schedule of twenty five days. This line was well equipped with more than a hundred specially constructed Concord coaches, a thousand horses, seven hundred mules, and about one hundred and fifty drivers. It received from the Government a subsidy of $600,000 a year, and was the longest continuous horse-express line then in existence on the North American continent. Until the outbreak of the Civil War, this southern route was the main artery of travel from the eastern States to the Pacific Coast; and it is estimated that, between 1849 and 1860, eight thousand emigrants crossed the Colorado Desert on their way to California.

Of all these eight thousand gold-seekers or pioneers, only one seems to have been impressed by the agricultural possibilities of the Salton Sink. Dr. O. M. Wozencraft, who has been described as "a man of marked personality and far-reaching vision who lived a generation before his time," crossed the Sink on his way to San Bernardino sometime in the early fifties; noticed the deposit of silt in the bed of the ancient lake; observed that the shallow basin lay so far below the level of the Colorado River that it might easily be irrigated therefrom; and reached the conclusion, previously stated by Professor Blake, that the arid waste of the Sink, if adequately supplied with water, could be made to "yield crops of almost any kind." This idea so took possession of his mind that, during the next five or six years, he spent much of his time and a large part of his private means in promoting schemes for the irrigation of this desert area. His engineer, Ebenezer Hadley of San Diego, made a preliminary survey of the Sink, and recommended a canal location practically identical with that which forty years later was adopted. In 1859, upon the initiative of Dr. Wozencraft, the California legislature asked Congress to cede to the State 3,000,000 acres of arid land, including the Salton Sink, for irrigation purposes. The bill was favorably reported by a House committee, but failed to pass. The Congressmen of that time regarded the reclamation of the Colorado Desert as a subject for jocular rather than serious treatment, and most of them were in sympathy with the California humorist, J. Ross Browne, who said: "I can see no great obstacle to success except the porous nature of the sand. By removing the sand from the desert, success would be insured at once."

With the failure of Dr. Wozencraft's attempt

to bring about the reclamation of the Colorado Desert, interest in that region gradually waned. The Butterfield Overland Mail service to the Pacific Coast was discontinued; a new "Pony Express" line to San Francisco, by way of Salt Lake City, was established; and before 1865, the southern route, via Yuma and the Colorado Desert, had been practically abandoned. Dr. Wozencraft continued talking, to all who would listen, about his scheme for the irrigation of the Salton Sink; but most people regarded it as visionary, and nobody seemed inclined to take it up. Only in 1891, thirty eight years after Professor Blake first suggested irrigation, and twenty nine years after Dr. Wozencraft's bill failed in Congress, was a serious attempt made to realize the "dream" of turning water into the Salton Sink and creating a fertile oasis in the heart of the Colorado Desert.

THE CREATION OF THE OASIS

In 1891, John C. Beatty, of California, another man who had imagination and foresight, became interested in the agricultural possibilities of the Colorado Desert, and formed a corporation under the name of "The California Irrigation Company" for the purpose of carry-

Relief Map of Imperial Valley and Its Environment

THE SALTON SEA

ing water into the Salton Sink from the Colorado River. He engaged as his technical adviser Mr. C. R. Rockwood, who had been in the employ of the U. S. Reclamation Service, and who was regarded as "a shrewd and clever man and engineer."[1] Mr. Rockwood made a careful survey of the Colorado delta, and found, as Lieutenant Bergland had found in an earlier survey, that between the river and the Sink there was a natural obstacle in the shape of a range of sand hills, which extended southward to the border line of Mexico. All natural overflows of the river, in prehistoric times, had been south of this barrier, and Mr. Rockwood thought that it would be easier and more economical to follow the river's ancient track than to put a conduit through these hills on the American side of the boundary. He proposed, therefore, to take water from the Colorado at Potholes, twelve miles above Yuma, carry it southward into Mexico, thence westward around the promontory of sand hills, and finally northward, across the line again, into southern California. This plan would involve the digging of a curving canal, forty or fifty miles in length, through Mexican territory; but it would obviate the necessity of cutting through

[1] Mr. H. T. Cory.

THE SALTON SEA

the sand hills, and would perhaps enable the diggers to utilize, on the Mexican side, one of the dry barrancas, or ancient overflow channels, through which the Colorado discharged into the Sink in ages past.

Owing to the lack of public confidence in reclamation experiments, Mr. Beatty and his associates were not able to secure as much capital as they needed for their enterprise, and when the monetary panic of 1893 came, they found themselves involved in financial difficulties from which they could not extricate themselves. In the latter part of 1893 the California Irrigation Co. went into bankruptcy, and its maps, records, and engineering data were turned over to Mr. Rockwood, in satisfaction of a judgment that he obtained in a suit for his unpaid salary.[1]

This seemed likely to put an end to the Salton Sink project; but Mr. Rockwood, whose observations and work in the Colorado delta had given him unbounded faith in the ultimate success of the scheme, determined to undertake the promotion of it himself. After several years of endeavor, he succeeded in forming another organization which was incorporated in New Jersey, on the 21st of April 1896, under

[1] Mr. Cory.

THE SALTON SEA

the title of "The California Development Company." For two years or more, this corporation tried to get permission from the Mexican Government to hold land, acquire rights, and dig an irrigating canal south of the boundary line; but the Mexican authorities refused to make any concessions, and it was finally found necessary to organize a subsidiary Mexican company. This corporation, which had a nominal capital of $62,000, was wholly owned and controlled by the California Development Co., but it operated under a Mexican charter.

As the financial resources of both companies were largely on paper, it then became necessary to secure real capital for the prosecution of the work, and this task Mr. Rockwood found extremely difficult. The proposed reclamation of an arid desert, where the thermometer went in summer to 120 in the shade, and where only two or three inches of rain fell in the course of the whole year, did not strike Eastern capitalists as a very promising venture, and most of them were disinclined to go into it. At last, however, in 1898, Mr. Rockwood secured a promise from certain capitalists in New York that they would advance the necessary funds; but two days before the papers were to be signed, the American battleship "Maine" was blown up in the harbor of Havana, and this catastrophe, together with the war that followed it, put an end to the negotiations.

But the plan for the irrigation of the Salton Sink was not destined to fail. Among the men with whom Dr. Wozencraft discussed it, in the early eighties, was George Chaffey, a civil engineer and irrigation expert of Los Angeles, who had had a good deal of experience in dealing with water problems, and who had already established successful irrigation systems in other parts of California.[1] Mr. Chaffey declined to go into it at Dr. Wozencraft's solicitation, not because he was afraid of the engineering difficulties involved, but because he thought that

---

[1] In his "Imperial Valley and Salton Sink," Mr. H. T. Cory, formerly chief engineer of the California Development Co., refers to Mr. Chaffey in the following words:

"The writer takes pleasure in expressing appreciation of the standing of Mr. George M. Chaffey in irrigation work in the West. The Ontario Colony he founded in 1883 was selected ten years later as a model for the irrigation exhibit at the World's Exposition, and in his work at Mildura, Australia, he designed, had built in England, and installed, the first centrifugal pumps on the same shaft with a total capacity of 320 cubic feet per second lifted 20 feet. He is at present, among other things, head of the magnificent water system irrigating 10,000 acres of citrus lands near Whittier, California, including the highest priced agricultural lands in California ($5,000 per acre). Furthermore he is a man of affairs, and of large means which he acquired principally in irrigation enterprises and banking."

the torrid climate of the Sink would prevent colonization of it, even if the colonists were promised plenty of water. Most men, he reasoned, would be frightened by the prospect of having to do hard agricultural labor in shade temperatures of 110 to 120, and sun temperatures of perhaps 140 to 150. They simply would not go to a place where they would be subjected to such heat. Some years later, however, Mr. Chaffey carried through successfully an irrigation enterprise in the interior of Australia, where the temperature in the shade often reached a maximum of 125, but where, nevertheless, men were able to work without danger or serious inconvenience. This changed his view of irrigation in the Colorado Desert; and in 1900, when the California Development Co. seemed unable to get money enough for its project elsewhere, Mr. Chaffey offered to finance the undertaking and superintend the work. His proposals were accepted, and on the 3rd of April 1900, he became president of the company, and signed a contract by which he bound himself to construct canals, at a cost of not more than $150,000, which would carry to the Imperial Valley 400,000 acre-feet of water per annum.[1]

Mr. Chaffey and his associates modified the

[1] Andrew M. Chaffey.

plan of Mr. Rockwood by taking water from the Colorado at Pilot Knob, nearly opposite Yuma, instead of at Potholes, twelve miles above. Putting in a head-gate there, they carried their main canal southward across the Mexican boundary, in a course nearly parallel with the river, until they reached the barranca, or dry overflow channel, known as the Alamo. As this ancient watercourse meandered westward in the direction of the Salton Sink, they were able to clear it out, enlarge it, and utilize most of it as a part of their irrigation system. Then, at a point about forty miles west of the Colorado, they carried their canal northward, across the boundary line again, into southern California. The work throughout was pushed with great energy, and on the 14th of May, 1901, a little more than a year after Mr. Chaffey assumed direction of affairs, water was turned in at the Pilot Knob head-gate, and the irrigation of the Salton Sink became a certainty, if not a fully accomplished fact.

As the California Development Co. was a water-selling company only, and had no proprietary interest in the lands to be irrigated, it was thought best to form another organization for the promotion of settlement; and in March 1901 the Imperial Land Company was incor-

THE SALTON SEA

porated for the purpose of attracting colonists, laying out town sites, and developing the Sink by bringing its lands into cultivation. Then Mr. Chaffey and the Land Company began an advertising campaign for the purpose of interesting the general public in the scheme; and in order not to frighten settlers and small investors by using in their advertisements and circulars the ominous words "desert" and "Sink," they changed the name of the basin that they proposed to irrigate and called it "The Imperial Valley." This title was evidently alluring, because it attracted small investors in all parts of the East, and particularly in New England. The Development Company's stock was bought, for example, in places as far away from the Salton Sink as Boston, Concord, Hopedale and Waverley, Mass.; Barre and Montpelier, Vt.; Portsmouth, N. H.; Elgin, Ill.; Portland, Oregon; and Toronto, Canada.[1] Settlers soon began to come in; mutual water companies were organized; and before the 3rd of April 1902, when Mr. Chaffey severed his connection with the company, four hundred miles of irrigating ditches had been dug, and water was available for 100,000 acres or more of irrigable land.[2]

[1] List of stockholders in Sou. Pac. office, N. Y.
[2] Andrew M. Chaffey.

THE SALTON SEA

About this time, however, the future of the Valley was seriously imperilled by unfavorable reports concerning its soil. In the early part of 1902, the Bureau of Soils of the U. S. Agricultural Department published the results of a survey of the irrigable lands in the Colorado Desert, and reported that they were so impregnated with alkali that very few things could be successfully grown on them.

"One hundred and twenty five thousand acres of land" (the report said) "have already been taken up by prospective settlers, many of whom talk of planting crops which it will be absolutely impossible to grow. They must early find that it will be useless to attempt their growth. . . . No doubt the best thing to do is to raise such crops as sugar beet, sorghum, and date palm (if the climate will permit), that are suited to such alkali conditions, and abandon as worthless the lands which contain too much alkali to grow those crops." ("Field Operations of the Bureau of Soils, U. S. Department of Agriculture," 1901, p. 587.)

This report, which was widely quoted and commented upon, acted as a serious check to the colonization of the Valley; and if it had been made two or three years earlier, it might have been fatal to the whole irrigation project. Fortunately, however, the crops raised by a few

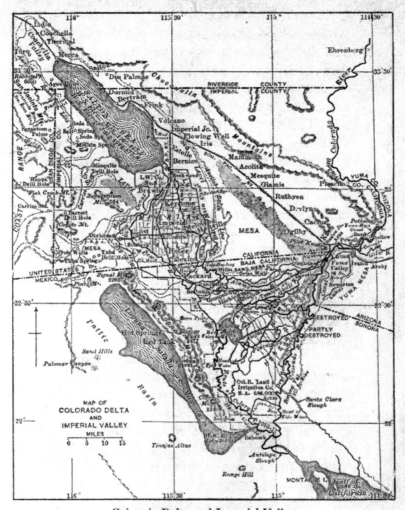

Colorado Delta and Imperial Valley

farmers who had already been cultivating this "alkali impregnated" land proved conclusively that the report of the analysis of the soil made by the Government experts was unduly pessimistic, if not wholly erroneous. Almost everything that was tried *did* grow, in spite of expert predictions, and the practical experience of men on the ground gradually revived public confidence in the productiveness of the irrigated lands. The colonization and development of the Valley then proceeded with great rapidity. The two thousand settlers on the ground at the end of 1902 increased to seven thousand in 1903 and to more than ten thousand in 1904. A branch of the Southern Pacific railroad was built through the Valley from Imperial Junction to Calexico and Mexicali; town sites were laid out in six or seven different places; the water system was extended by the digging of nearly four hundred additional miles of irrigating ditches and canals; and before the 1st of January 1905, one hundred and twenty thousand acres of reclaimed land were actually under cultivation, while two hundred thousand acres more had been covered by water stock.

The observed fertility of the soil completely discredited the reports of the Government experts, and more than justified the prediction

THE SALTON SEA

made by Professor Blake half a century before that when the Sink should be supplied with water, it would produce "crops of almost any kind." Grapes, melons and garden vegetables matured in the Valley earlier than in any other part of California; barley was a profitable crop; alfalfa could be cut five or six times a year; and the finest quality of long-staple Egyptian cotton yielded more than a bale (500 pounds) to the acre. Experiments proved also that the climate and soil were well adapted to the culture of grapes, grapefruit, oranges, lemons, olives, figs, dates, pomegranates, apricots, peaches and pears.

The fear that men would not be willing or able to do hard work in the hot climate of the valley proved to be wholly groundless. Great heat is not necessarily weakening or prostrating unless it is accompanied with great humidity, and the air of the Valley is at all seasons extremely dry. In a discussion of this subject, Mr. H. T. Cory, formerly chief engineer of the California Development Co., says:

"The climate of the region, with its long, hot, dry summers, is peculiarly favorable to agricultural luxuriance. Thus it is that here the very earliest grapes, fruits and vegetables are produced for the United States market, with the consequent advantage of commanding the highest prices. This is notably true of the Imperial Valley cantaloupe, now famous all over this country, and of the early grapes, asparagus etc. On account of the very low humidity and gentle winds which blow most of the time in hot weather, the sensible temperature—which is indicated by the wet-bulb thermometer readings and gives the measure of heat felt by the human body—is much less than the actual temperature as measured by the dry bulb. It is conservative to say that a temperature of 110 in Imperial Valley is not more uncomfortable than 95 in Los Angeles, or 85 in the more humid sections of the Eastern States. Furthermore the nights are always cool, the low humidity resulting in rapid and large daily temperature variations."

Under these favoring conditions of soil and climate, it seemed almost certain, in 1904, that the Imperial Valley would have a great and prosperous future; but no forecast in that region is trustworthy unless it takes into account the irrigating agency, as well as the climate and the soil. The Colorado River created the Salton Sink, and made fertile the Imperial Valley; but it could destroy, as well as create; and in 1904 it showed itself in a new aspect and threatened the Valley with a terrible calamity.

A Part of the Colorado River Watershed. The Grand Cañon

THE SALTON SEA

THE RUNAWAY RIVER

The most serious problem with which engineers have to deal in the irrigation of arid land from a turbid river is the getting rid of silt, and this problem is a particularly difficult one in the Imperial Valley, owing to the immense amount of sediment that the irrigating water contains. The Colorado River, until after it passes the Grand Canon, is almost everywhere a swift, turbulent stream, with great eroding capacity. As Mr. E. C. LaRue has said, in a brief but graphic description of it,

"When the snows melt in the Rocky and Wind River Mountains, a million cascade brooks unite to form a thousand torrent creeks; a thousand torrent creeks unite to form half a hundred rivers beset with cataracts; half a hundred roaring rivers unite to form the Colorado, which flows, a mad, turbid stream, into the Gulf of California." ("Colorado River and Its Utilization," a Geological Survey report, Government Printing Office, Washington 1916.)

Such a river, naturally, dissolves the earth and gnaws the rocks over which it tears its way, and takes up millions of tons of solid matter, in the shape of gravel, sand and finely pulverized soil. This great volume of sediment, when

THE SALTON SEA

finally dropped, not only tends to change the river's course by creating bars at or near its mouth, but gradually fills up the irrigating ditches and canals and thus lessens their carrying capacity. A single day's supply of water for the Imperial Valley contains silt enough to make a levee twenty feet high, twenty feet wide, and one mile long. (Imperial Valley Press, July 25 1916). If this silt is not dredged out, sluiced out, or collected in a settling basin, it eventually raises the beds of the canals, fills the ditches, and chokes up the whole irrigation system.

The managers of the California Development Co. had difficulty, almost from the first, in keeping their waterways open. As more and more land was brought into cultivation, more and more water was required, while the silting up of the canals lessened the ability of the company to meet the constantly increasing demand. There was a shortage as early as the winter of 1902-3; but the situation did not become serious until the following year, when the main canal, for a distance of four miles below the intake, became so silted up that it could not possibly carry the volume of water that was imperatively needed. An attempt was made to remedy this state of affairs by putting in a waste-gate, eight miles below the intake, for the purpose of sluicing out the channel in time of high water.

"The idea" (as stated by Mr. Cory) "was to divert a large quantity of water during the flood season, waste it through the Best waste-gate, and in this way scour out the upper portion of the canal. At first, the action was as expected, and some two feet in the bottom were carried away. When, however, the river reached its maximum height, . . . and carried an excessive silt content, especially of the heavier and sandy type, this scouring action was entirely overcome, and the bottom of this stretch was raised approximately one foot higher than during the previous year."

This silting up of the main canal, and the consequent reduction of its carrying capacity, caused great injury to the agricultural interests of the Valley. Crops in many places perished for lack of water, and hundreds of farmers put in damage claims, which amounted in the aggregate to half a million dollars. In the late summer of 1904, it became evident that radical measures would have to be taken at once to increase the water supply. As the managers of the company had neither the financial means nor the requisite machinery for quickly dredging out the silted part of the canal, they decided,

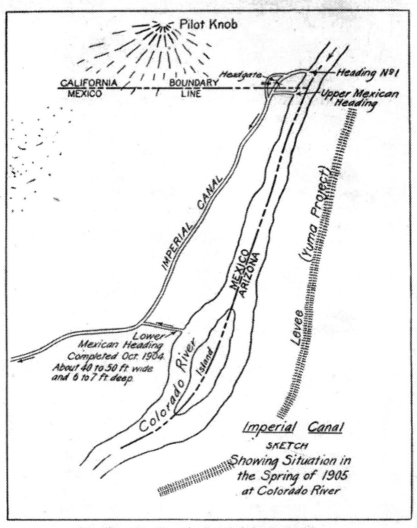

The Three Headings (or Intakes), in Spring of 1905

THE SALTON SEA

in September of that year, to cut a new intake from the river at a point about four miles south of the international boundary. This would eliminate the choked-up part of the canal, and let water directly into the part that was unobstructed.

If President Heber and Chief Engineer Rockwood had been aware of the fact that the Colorado was even then preparing to pour its waters into the Salton Sink, by making one of its semi-millennial changes of course, they might perhaps have fortified the western bank instead of cutting through it; but there was little or nothing to show the extreme instability of the conditions that were then determining the trend of the river across its delta, and the idea that it might burst through this intake and again turn the Valley into a fresh-water lake does not seem to have occurred to anyone. The cutting was therefore made and the water shortage relieved; but at the cost of imminent peril to the whole Valley and its twelve thousand inhabitants.

In view of the tremendous and disastrous consequences of this measure, it is only fair that Chief Engineer Rockwood should be allowed to state, with some fullness, his reasons for adopting it, and for failing to put in a headgate to control the flow of water through the channel and thus prevent its enlargement. In an article entitled "Born of the Desert," published in the second annual magazine number of the Calexico Chronicle, in May 1909, he sets forth his reasons in the following words:

" As soon as the summer flood (1904) dropped, I discovered that instead of the bottom" (of the canal) "being lower, it was approximately one foot above that of the year previous. . . . We knew that with the dredging tools which we had it would be impossible to dredge out this four miles of canal in sufficient time for the uses of the Valley, providing the water in the river should drop as low as it had the previous year. . . . We were then confronted with the proposition of doing one of two things, either cutting a new heading from the canal to the river below the silted four-mile section of the canal, or else allowing the Valley to pass through another winter with an insufficient water supply. The latter proposition we could not face, for the reason that the people of the Valley had an absolute right to demand that water should be furnished them, and it was questionable in our minds as to whether we would be able to keep out of bankruptcy if we were to be confronted by another period of shortage in the coming season of 1904–1905.

"The cutting of the lower intake, after mature deliberation, and upon the insistence of several of the leading men of the Valley, was decided upon. We hesitated about making this cut, not so much because we believed we were incurring danger of the river's breaking through, as from the fact that we had been unable to obtain the consent of the Government of Mexico to make it, and we believed that we were jeopardizing our Mexican rights should the cut be made without the consent of the Government. On a telegraphic communication, however, from our attorney in the City of Mexico, to go ahead and make the cut, we did so, under the presumption that he had obtained the necessary permit from the Mexican authorities. It was some time after this, in fact after the cut was made in the river, before we discovered that he had been unable to obtain the formal permit, but had simply obtained the promise of certain officials that we would not be interfered with, providing that plans were at once submitted for the necessary controlling structures to be placed in this heading.

". . . In cutting from the main canal to the river at this point, we had to dredge a distance of 3300 feet only, through easy material to remove, while an attempt to dredge out the main canal above would have meant the dredging of four miles of very difficult material. We began the cut the latter end of September and completed it in about three weeks. As soon as the cut was decided upon, elaborate plans for a controlling gate were immediately started, and when completed, early in November, were immediately forwarded to the City of Mexico for

THE SALTON SEA

the approval of the engineers of the Mexican Government, without whose approval we had no authority or right to construct the gate. Notwithstanding the insistence of our attorney in the City of Mexico, and various telegraphic communications insisting upon this approval being hurried, we were unable to obtain it until twelve months afterward, namely, the month of December 1905.

"In the meantime, serious trouble had begun. We have since been accused of gross negligence and criminal carelessness in making this cut; but I doubt as to whether anyone should be accused of negligence, or carelessness, in failing to foresee what had never happened before. We had before us at the time the history of the river as shown by the rod-readings kept at Yuma for a period of twenty seven years. In the twenty seven years there had been but three winter floods. In no winter of the twenty seven had there been two winter floods. It was not probable, then, that there would be any winter flood to enlarge the cut made by us, and without doubt, as it seemed to us, we would be able to close the cut, before the approach of the summer flood, by the same means that we had used in closing the cut for three successive years around the Chaffey gate at the head of the canal.[1] During this winter of 1905,

---

[1] The sill of the Chaffey gate proved to be too high for low stages of water, and a canal, at a lower level, was cut around the structure and closed every year with a brush-and-earth dam before the approach of the summer flood. G. K.

THE SALTON SEA

however, we had more than one winter flood. The first flood came, I believe, about the first of February, but did not enlarge the lower intake. On the contrary, it caused such a silt deposit in the lower intake that I found it necessary, after the flood had passed, to put the dredge through in order to deepen the channel sufficiently to allow water to come into the valley for the use of the people. This was followed shortly by another heavy flood that did not erode the banks of the intake, but, on the contrary, the same as the first, caused a deposit of silt and a necessary dredging. We were not alarmed by these floods, as it was still very early in the season. No damage had been done by them, and we still believed that there would be no difficulty in closing the intake before the approach of the summer flood, which was the only one we feared. However, the first two floods were followed by a third, coming sometime in March, and this was sufficient notice to us that we were up against a very unusual season, something unknown in the history of the river as far back as we were able to reach; and as it was now approaching the season of the year when we might reasonably expect the river surface to remain at an elevation that would allow sufficient water for the uses of the Valley to be gotten through the upper intake, we decided to close the lower." ("Born of the Desert," by C. R. Rockwood, Calexico Chronicle, May 1909.)

THE SALTON SEA

At the time when the first attempt to close the intake was made, the cutting was about sixty feet wide. A dam of piles, brush and sandbags was thrown across it in March 1905, but it had hardly been completed when another flood came down the Colorado and swept it away. A second dam of the same kind, built a few weeks later, shared the same fate. By the middle of June, the river was discharging 90,000 cubic feet of water per second; the width of the lower intake had increased from sixty feet to one hundred and sixty; water was overflowing the banks of the main canal and accumulating in the deepest part of the Sink; and a new Salton Sea was in process of formation.

Such was the state of affairs when Mr. Harriman and the Southern Pacific Railroad Company first became directly interested in the problem of river control. Early in 1905, the California Development Co., finding itself in pecuniary difficulties, applied to Mr. Julius Kruttschnitt, General Manager of the Southern Pacific, for a loan, on the alleged ground that the Imperial Valley was furnishing a great deal of traffic to the railroad, and the irrigation company was therefore warranted in asking for financial assistance. Mr. Kruttschnitt, however, declined to consider the application. The

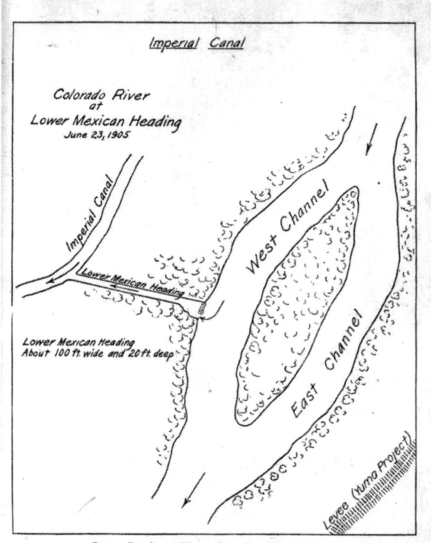

Lower Intake at Time of Southern Pacific Loan

petitioners then addressed the President of the railroad company, Mr. E. H. Harriman, who, it was thought, might be induced to give the necessary aid, even though he had no personal interest in the Valley and no connection whatever with the California Development Co. Mr. Harriman, as a man of imagination and far-seeing vision, was naturally in sympathy with the bold attempt to irrigate and reclaim the arid lands of the Colorado Desert, and when the matter of the loan was presented to him, he not only gave it immediate consideration, but ordered an investigation and a report. He finally consented, against the advice of Mr. Kruttschnitt and other counsellors, to loan the Development Company $200,000, "to be used in paying off certain of its floating indebtedness and in completing and perfecting its canal system." Inasmuch, however, as the financial management of the irrigation company had not always been judicious, Mr. Harriman and the Southern Pacific stipulated that they should have the right to select three of its directors, one of whom should be president, and that fifty one per cent of its stock (6300 shares) should be placed in the hands of a trustee as collateral security for the loan. This stipulation was agreed to, and on the 20th of June 1905, the Southern

THE SALTON SEA

Pacific Company, as chief creditor, took temporary control of the California Development Company by selecting three of its directors, and by appointing as its president Mr. Epes Randolph, of Tucson, who was then acting also as president of the Harriman Lines in Arizona and Mexico.[1]

When Mr. Harriman and the Southern Pacific thus took over the management of the California Development Company, they had no intention of assuming its responsibilities, directing its engineering work, or deriving revenue from its operations. All they aimed to do was to see that the money loaned was

---

[1] Mr. Randolph was a distinguished civil engineer and railroad manager, who had been, at one time, superintendent of the Tucson division of the Southern Pacific under Mr. C. P. Huntington. After the latter's death, he went to Los Angeles, where he built and managed Mr. H. E. Huntington's interurban system of electric railways and where he made the acquaintance of Mr. Harriman. Finding that his health would not permit him to live in the climate of Los Angeles, he returned in 1904 to Arizona, where he was appointed president of the Arizona Eastern Railroad Company and the Southern Pacific Railroad Company of Mexico—Harriman lines. Mr. Randolph, at that time, was regarded as one of the ablest civil engineers in the United States, and he had already had much experience in dealing with river-control problems in the South. He was also one of Mr. Harriman's most trusted counsellors, and it was upon his recommendation that the Southern Pacific Company's lines were extended into Mexico.

honestly and judiciously spent. The financial management of the company, had not previously been above criticism, to say the least; and Mr. Harriman was fully justified in taking such control as might be necessary to ensure proper expenditure of the funds that the Southern Pacific Company furnished. From the representations made by the Development Company at that time, it was thought that the lower Mexican intake might be closed at a cost of not more than $20,000, and the Company proposed to use the remainder of the $200,000 loan in "completing and perfecting its canal system," under the direction of its own technical experts. When, however, President Randolph made a personal investigation of the state of affairs, shortly after his appointment, he found the situation much more serious than the Development Company had represented it to be, and telegraphed Mr. Harriman that the Imperial Valley could not be saved by the expenditure of $200,000. To control the river, he said, under the conditions then existing, would be extremely difficult. Nobody could foresee what would be the ultimate cost of the engineering operations, but it "might easily run into three quarters of a million dollars."

Mr. Harriman could have insisted, even then,

upon a return of the unspent loan, and could have withdrawn from the financially hazardous undertaking; but instead of doing this, he telegraphed President Randolph: "Are you certain you can put the river back into the old channel?" Mr. Randolph replied: "I am certain that it can be done." Then wired Mr. Harriman: "Go ahead and do it."

As Chief Engineer Rockwood was thought to be familiar with the problem of river control, and quite competent to deal with it, he was allowed, at first, to take such measures for closing the intake as seemed to him best. He had made the cutting long before the Southern Pacific had anything to do with the irrigation of the Valley, and upon him, primarily, devolved the responsibility of averting consequences that might be disastrous.

Although the Mexican cutting, at that time, had virtually become a crevasse, the flow through it was not great enough to endanger the cultivated lands of the valley. The excess of water overflowed the banks of the canal—the old Alamo barranca—but it ran into the deepest part of the Sink, where it slowly accumulated without flooding anything except the works of the New Liverpool Salt Company. Civil Engineer C. E. Grunsky, of the U. S. Reclamation

Service, who made an inspection of the intake three days after the loan to the California Development Company, described the situation as "not serious, but sufficiently alarming to require some attention." The most disquieting feature of it was the steepness of the incline toward the Imperial Valley as compared with that toward the Gulf of California. The fall of the Colorado from the intake to the Gulf was only one hundred feet, while that from the intake to the bottom of the Valley was nearly four hundred feet. As the distance was about the same, either way, the Valley incline was approximately four times as steep as the river-bed incline, and if the whole stream should break through the intake and go down the steeper slope, the velocity of the current would make the stopping of it extremely difficult, if not absolutely impossible. When a turbulent river, in flood, discharges at the rate of 100,000 cubic feet per second down an easily eroded and comparatively steep declivity into an immense basin four hundred feet deep, it soon gets beyond control.

The difficulty of dealing with these conditions was greatly increased by the impossibility of predicting or anticipating floods. The annual rise of the Colorado, above its junction

THE SALTON SEA

with the Gila, begins in the spring, reaches its maximum in July, and subsides to normal about the middle of August. This period of high water is fairly regular and may be counted upon. Floods in the drainage basin of the Gila, however, are capricious, occur at all seasons of the year, and are particularly violent in the fall and winter months. "These floods," as Mr. Cory says, "are far more to be feared and reckoned with, in preparing and conducting engineering work along the lower Colorado River, than anything coming down the Colorado River proper," partly because they come suddenly and unexpectedly, and partly because they carry immense quantities of driftwood. During the Gila flood of November 29–30, 1905, the water at Yuma rose ten feet in ten hours, with a maximum discharge of 102,000 cubic feet per second, while driftwood almost completely covered the water surface. Such floods, coming with little or no warning, are almost irresistible.

When, in July 1905, the summer flood in the Colorado began to subside, Chief Engineer Rockwood determined to fend off the main current, and lessen the pressure on the crevasse, by means of a jetty. Just opposite the intake was a bush-overgrown island, five eighths of a mile long by a quarter of a mile wide, which split the river into two channels. Across the western channel, from the head of the island to the bank, a semi-barrier was built, of piling, barbed wire and brush. This obstruction, it was thought, might check the flow into the western channel, cause a deposit of heavy silt, and eventually create a bar which would deflect the main current around the northern end of the island and thus carry it away from the mouth of the crevasse. The attempt was only partly successful. A bar was formed, but it did not completely close the channel, nor deflect the main current. There was still an opening, about one hundred and twenty five feet in width, through which the rush of water was so great that it could not be controlled. The attempt to deflect the main current into the eastern channel, by means of a jetty, was then abandoned.

Up to this time, the Southern Pacific Company had not taken part directly in the work of river control. After the failure of the jetty, however, in August 1905, President Randolph sent his assistant, Mr. H. T. Cory,[1] to the scene

---

[1] Mr. Cory was a talented civil engineer who had left his professorial chair in the engineering department of the University of Cincinnati to enter the service of the Southern

THE SALTON SEA

of operations, with instructions to confer with Chief Engineer Rockwood and ascertain what his views and intentions were. Mr. Rockwood, at that time, did not regard the situation as at all alarming. The flow through the crevasse, he said, was doing useful work in scouring out and deepening the main canal (the old Alamo barranca) and there was little danger that the whole river would go that way. He was not in favor of closing the enlarged intake altogether, because that would shut off the water supply of the Imperial Valley and cause more damage than was then being done by the river. The deeper part of the Salton Sink, he said, was a natural drainage basin, and as it was much below the zone of cultivation in the valley as a whole, the accumulation of water in it was not likely to do a great amount of damage.

"I told him," Mr. Cory says, "that I thought the situation was serious, even granting all he said were true; that he would better shut the break right away, for while the water might be doing good work in enlarging the canal of the California Development Company, the situa-

Pacific Railroad system. Just prior to this time—in May 1905—he had been appointed assistant to President Randolph, with headquarters at Tucson.

tion was dangerous; that it was playing with fire."

Throughout the month of August 1905, the intake continued to widen, with the caving away of its banks, and in September Mr. Harriman and President Randolph decided that another effort must be made either to close the break, or to regulate and control the flow of water through it. About the first of October, at the suggestion and under the supervision of Mr. E. S. Edinger, a Southern Pacific engineer, an attempt was made to close the channel west of the island by means of a six-hundred-foot barrier-dam of piling, brush-mattresses and sandbags. This dam, which was built in October and November at a cost of about $60,000, might perhaps have checked or lessened the flow through the crevasse if nothing unforeseen had happened; but on the 29th–30th of November a tremendous flood, carrying great masses of driftwood, came down the Gila and increased the discharge of the Colorado from 12,000 to 115,000 cubic feet per second. The dam could not withstand such pressure, and even before the peak of the flood was reached it went out altogether, leaving hardly a vestige behind. As a large part of the island was eroded and carried away at the same time,

THE SALTON SEA

further operations in this locality were regarded as impracticable. The crevasse had then widened to six hundred feet, and nearly the whole of the river poured through it into the deepest part of the Sink, where there was already a lake with a surface area of one hundred and fifty square miles. The main line of the Southern Pacific, in many places, was almost awash, and the whole population of the Valley was alarmed by the prospect of being drowned out. If the break could not be closed and the river brought under control before the period of high water in the spring and summer of 1906, it seemed more than probable that sixty miles of the Southern Pacific track would be submerged; that the irrigation system of the California Development Company would be destroyed; and that the whole basin of the Imperial Valley would ultimately become a fresh-water lake.

The difficulty of dealing with this menacing situation was greatly increased by the necessity of furnishing an uninterrupted supply of water to the farmers of the valley while engineering operations were in progress. It would not do to shut the river out altogether, because that would leave without irrigation nearly two hundred square miles of cultivated land. The

Colorado must be controlled, but not wholly excluded. Several methods of solving this problem were suggested, but the only two that seemed likely to succeed were advocated by Consulting Engineer Schuyler and Chief Engineer Rockwood. Mr. Schuyler proposed that a new steel-and-concrete head-gate be put in near Pilot Knob, where a solid rock foundation could be secured; that the four miles of silted channel be re-excavated and enlarged by a powerful steam dredge specially built for the purpose; and that the whole low-water flow of the river be then turned through this head-gate into the enlarged canal and thence into the Alamo barranca west of the break. By this means the settlers would be continuously supplied with water, while the crevasse-opening would be left dry enough to close with a permanent levee or dam. The whole work, it was thought, could be finished in three months, or at least before the coming of the next summer flood.

Chief Engineer Rockwood's plan also involved the building of a new head-gate, but he proposed to locate it on the northern side of the intake, and to carry the whole low-water flow of the river through it by means of an excavated by-pass. This, too, would keep the settlers

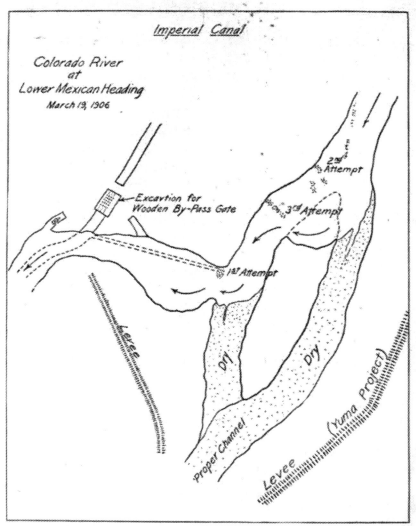

Lower Intake in Spring of 1906 (showing site of Rockwood head-gate and first three attempts to close the break)

supplied with water and leave the crevasse-opening dry while it was being closed. The chief objection to the latter plan was that the head-gate would necessarily be of wood, and would have to stand on a treacherous foundation of easily eroded silt which might possibly be undermined. Late in November, after full consideration, President Randolph decided to try both plans and to work on them simultaneously. Contracts for the structural steel and iron work for the concrete head-gate were let in Los Angeles; the machinery for the 850-ton floating dredge "Delta" was ordered in San Francisco; materials for the Rockwood head-gate were collected on the northern side of the intake, and work was pushed on all of these structures with the greatest possible energy throughout the winter. In spite, however, of all efforts, none of them could be finished in the allotted time. The steel-and-concrete head-gate was not completed until the 28th of June; the dredge "Delta," owing to the partial destruction of San Francisco, was not ready until the following November, and even the Rockwood gate, on which alternate shifts of men had worked night and day, was not in working order until the 18th of April. Meanwhile, the summer flood of 1906 had begun, with a discharge of

32,200 cubic feet per second through the crevasse. This flow would have exceeded the capacity of the Rockwood gate, even if it had been possible to turn the river through the by-pass that led to it, and the attempt to bring the Colorado under control was again temporarily abandoned.

Then a long series of misfortunes and catastrophes followed, one after another. On the 18th of April, 1906, San Francisco was partially destroyed by earthquake and fire, and Mr. Harriman hurried to the scene of the disaster for the purpose of affording help. President Randolph soon joined him there, and, at the first opportunity, described to him the almost desperate state of affairs in the Colorado delta. The California Development Company had used up the $200,000 loaned to it by the Southern Pacific the previous year; the river was still uncontrolled, and the impending flood threatened to inundate the Valley and deprive 12,000 people of their property and homes. Mr. Harriman was not a man to be daunted or "rattled" by a sudden and menacing emergency. "There, in the bustle and confusion of temporary offices, with the ruins of San Francisco still smoking, with the facilities of his roads taxed to the utmost in carrying people away from the stricken city, with the wonderful railway system which constituted his life work crippled to an unknown extent, and with the financial demands resulting from the disaster impossible to determine," he consented to advance an additional sum of $250,000 for controlling the Colorado River and protecting the Imperial Valley. "It has always seemed to me," writes Mr. Cory, "that this was really the most remarkable thing in the whole series of extraordinary happenings."

With the promise of this additional sum of $250,000, President Randolph returned to the Imperial Valley to take up again the fight with the runaway river. The flood, at that time, was steadily rising; the width of the crevasse had increased to a quarter of a mile, and the Colorado was pouring into the Salton basin more than four billion cubic feet of water every twenty four hours.

On the 19th of April, 1906, the day after the San Francisco earthquake, Mr. C. R. Rockwood, who had been the chief engineer of the California Development Company for about four years, tendered his resignation, and Mr. H. T. Cory, President Randolph's assistant, was appointed in his place. The Southern Pacific Company then assumed full control and direction of defensive operations, and all sub-

A Flood Waterfall in Imperial Valley, Cutting Back

Nearer View of Flood Cataract in Imperial Valley, Cutting Back

sequent work was planned and executed by its engineers, with the powerful support of Mr. Harriman and his great railway system.

The task set before Messrs. Randolph, Cory, Hind and Clarke was one that might well have daunted even engineers of their great ability and experience. As the summer flood approached its maximum, in the latter part of June, the crevasse widened to more than half a mile, and the whole river, rushing through the break, spread out over an area eight or ten miles in width, and then, collecting in separate streams as it ran down the slope of the basin, discharged at last into the Salton Sea through the flooded channel of the New River barranca. Thousands of acres of land, covered with growing crops, were inundated, and thousands of acres more were so eroded and furrowed by the torrential streams that they never could be cultivated again. The works of the New Liverpool Salt Company were buried under sixty feet of water; the towns of Calexico and Mexicali were partially destroyed, and in many places the tracks of the Inter-California Railroad (a branch of the Southern Pacific) and the Holtville Interurban were deeply submerged or wholly carried away. The wooden flumes which carried the irrigating water over

THE SALTON SEA

the New River barranca were swept down into the Salton Sea, and 30,000 acres of cultivated land in the western part of the Valley became dry, barren and uninhabitable. At the height of the flood, the Colorado discharged through the crevasse more than 75,000 cubic feet of water per second, or six billion cubic feet every twenty four hours, while the Salton Sea, into which this immense volume of water was poured, rose at the rate of seven inches per day over an area of four hundred square miles. The main line of the Southern Pacific was soon inundated, and five times in the course of the summer the company had to move its track to higher ground.

The most dangerous and alarming feature of the situation was the "cutting back" of the torrents into which the flood-water collected as it rushed down the delta slope toward the Salton Sea. The fine silt of which the soil was composed washed out like powdered sugar, and wherever there happened to be a strong current, the flow soon produced a miniature rapid. The rapid then became a cascade, the cascade grew into a fall, and the fall finally developed into a roaring cataract, which "cut back," up-stream, at the rate sometimes of four thousand feet a day, widening as it receded, and leaving below it a deep gorge with almost per-

Agricultural Sands Eroded and Destroyed by Flood Water

THE SALTON SEA

pendicular walls. Some of the gorges eroded in the light friable silt by these receding waterfalls were fifty to eighty feet deep and more than a thousand feet across. It was estimated that the channels thus formed during the floods of 1906 had an aggregate length of more than forty miles, and that the solid matter scoured out of them and carried down into the Salton Sea was nearly four times as great as the whole amount excavated in the digging of the Panama Canal. But the damage actually done by these receding waterfalls was unimportant in comparison with the damage that they threatened to do. If one of them should "cut back" far enough to break into the irrigation system of the California Development Company, all the water in the latter's canals and ditches would instantly flow down into the deep gorge below the cataract, and bring about a disaster almost unprecedented in history. The twelve thousand settlers in the desert oasis were wholly dependent upon the irrigation system for their supply of drinking water, and if that supply should be cut off, they would be compelled by thirst either to camp around the margin of the Salton Sea, which was ten or fifteen miles away from most of them, or else get out of the valley within forty eight hours

THE SALTON SEA

in a wild precipitate stampede. Paradoxical as it may seem, the danger of being driven out by lack of water was even greater and more immediate than the danger of being drowned out by the rising flood.

The changes in the topography of the Colorado delta brought about by the crevasse and the floods of 1906 were greater than any that had occurred there in the three preceding centuries of recorded history. In referring to them Mr. Cory says:

"The effect of this flood, in a geological way, was of extraordinary interest and very spectacular. In nine months, the runaway waters of the Colorado had eroded from the New and Alamo River channels and carried down into the Salton Sea a yardage almost four times as great as that of the entire Panama Canal. The combined length of the channels cut out was almost forty three miles, the average width being one thousand feet and the depth fifty feet. To this total of 400,000,000 to 450,000,000 cubic yards must be added almost ten per cent for side cañons, surface erosions etc. Very rarely, if ever before, has it been possible to see a geological agency effect in a few months a change which usually requires centuries."

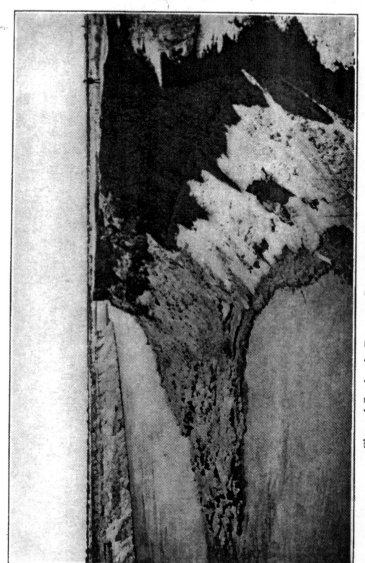

Channel Cut by the Runaway River on Its Way to the Salton Sea

THE SALTON SEA

THE SAVING OF THE VALLEY

When the Southern Pacific engineers undertook to avert the peril that menaced the Imperial Valley in the summer of 1906, they found little in recorded history to help or guide them. Inundations, of course, had often occurred before, on the Mississippi River and its tributaries, in the valley of "China's Sorrow," and in many other parts of the world; but these floods were merely overflows on a relatively flat surface. The cosmical plunge of a great river into the dried-up basin of an ancient sea was an unprecedented phenomenon, and one which raised engineering problems that were wholly new. Nobody had ever before tried to control a rush of 360,000,000 cubic feet of water per hour, down a four-hundred-foot slope of easily eroded silt, into a basin big enough to hold Long Island Sound. There was nothing in the past experience of the world that could suggest a practicable method of dealing with such conditions. Neither was much help to be obtained from the advice of hydraulic experts. Of the forty or fifty eminent engineers who visited the Colorado delta in 1905 and 1906, hardly any two agreed upon a definite plan of defensive work, while almost everyone found something objectionable in the measures suggested by others. All admitted, however, that "the situation was a desperate one;" that it was "without engineering parallel;" and that "there seemed to be only a fighting chance of controlling the river."

Mr. Harriman, who believed and who once said that "nothing is impossible," never doubted that the control of the Colorado River was within human power and human resources. In building the Lucin cut-off across the Great Salt Lake of Utah he had successfully carried through one "impossible" enterprise, and he did not hesitate to undertake another. Inspired by his invincible courage, President Randolph and his engineers set about their herculean task.

In preparing for a fifth attempt to bring the Colorado under control, they determined to modify the plan of operations previously followed by substituting rock for the materials that had before been used in the construction of dams. Practical experience had shown that piling, brush, sandbags and earth could not be made to support the pressure of the river in full flood, while a series of rock-fill barrier dams, of sufficient width and height, might be strong enough to stand even a flood discharge of

THE SALTON SEA

115,000 cubic feet of water per second. In making this change of plan, Mr. Randolph acted on his own judgment and in direct opposition to the views and advice of experts who were acquainted with the situation. Almost all of the engineers who had visited the break, including many of national and international reputation, regarded a rock-fill barrier dam as wholly unworthy of consideration, for at least two reasons. First, the rock would probably sink into the soft silt bottom, and keep on going down indefinitely. It might perhaps be supported by a strong brush-mattress foundation, but even then, the mattress would be likely to break under the weight of the load and thus fail to answer its purpose. Second, the water going over a rock-fill dam, while it was in course of construction, would almost certainly wash away some one rock at the top. This, by increasing the overflow at that point, would dislodge more rocks, and finally create a breach that could not be closed. President Randolph who had used brush-mattresses and rock-fill dams on the Tombigbee River in Alabama many years before, fully considered these objections but did not find them convincing and steadfastly adhered to his own plan.

The preparations made for the summer's

work were far more thorough and comprehensive than any that had ever been made before. Realizing the importance of adequate transportation, President Randolph and his engineers immediately began the construction of a branch railroad from the main line of the Southern Pacific to the scene of operations at the crêvasse, with ample sidings and terminal facilities at both ends. Then they borrowed from the Union Pacific three hundred of the mammoth side-dump cars known as "battleships," which had been used in the construction of the Lucin cut-off, and which had a carrying capacity of fifty or sixty tons each. The California Development Company had three light-draught steamers and a number of barges that could be used on the river, and the Southern Pacific Company furnished complete work-trains, from time to time, until a maximum of ten was reached. The next requisite was material for levees and dams, and this they secured by drawing upon all the rock quarries within a radius of four hundred miles, and by opening a new one, with a face of six hundred feet and a height of forty feet, on the granite ledge at Andrade near the concrete head-gate. Clay they obtained from a deposit just north of the Mexican boundary, and gravel they hauled from the Southern Pacific Company's "Mam-

THE SALTON SEA

moth Gravel Pit," which was situated on the main line about forty miles west of the crevasse spur. From Los Angeles they brought 1100 ninety-foot piles, 19,000 feet of heavy timbers for railway trestles, and forty miles of steel cable to be used in the weaving of brush-mattresses. The Southern Pacific Company furnished pile-drivers, steam shovels for the granite quarry and gravel pit, several carloads of repair parts, and a large quantity of stores and materials of various kinds. It also detailed for service on the spur railroad and at the crevasse as many engineers, mechanics and skilled workmen as were needed. The chief reason, Mr. Cory says, "for having the railroad company supply so great a quantity of labor, equipment and supplies, was that it afforded an opportunity to assemble quickly a thoroughly organized and efficient force of men; the advantage of obtaining material and supplies through the purchasing department of the Harriman systems; immediate shipment of repair parts not kept on hand; and the ability to increase or decrease rapidly the force and equipment without confusion."

The requisite most difficult to obtain, in sufficient amount, was unskilled labor. An attempt was made to get five hundred peons

THE SALTON SEA

from central Mexico; but it did not succeed, and Mr. Cory was finally compelled to mobilize all the Indian tribes in that part of the Southwest—Pimas, Papagoes, Maricopas and Yumas from Arizona and Cocopahs and Diegueños from Mexico. These Indians fraternized and got along together amicably, and constituted with their families a separate camp of about two thousand people. The rest of the laborers were Mexicans from the vicinity, and drifting adventurers from all parts of the United States who were attracted to the place by the novelty of the work and the publicity given to it in the newspapers. Arrangements were made with the Mexican authorities to put the whole region under martial law and to send a force of rurales with a military commandant to police the camps.

Active work began on the 6th of August, 1906, when the summer flood had fallen enough to reduce the flow through the crevasse to about 24,000 cubic feet per second. By that time the receding water had left exposed extensive sandbars on both sides of the river, which narrowed the channel to 600 or 700 feet, and President Randolph's plan was to dam this channel sufficiently to throw all or most of the water through the by-pass and the Rockwood head-gate, and

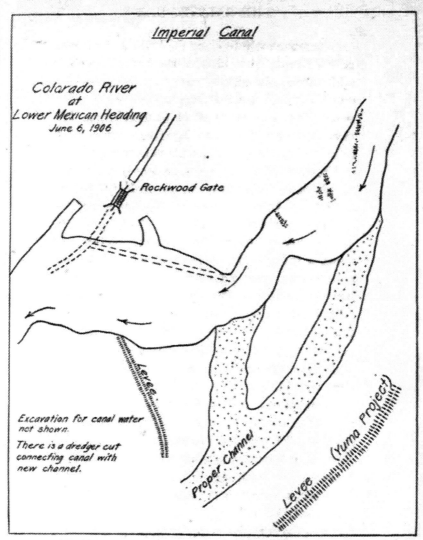

Situation in June, 1906 (whole river going into Salton Sink)

THE SALTON SEA

then permanently to close the break. As it was deemed essential to blanket the bed of the river with a woven brush-mattress, to prevent bottom erosion and to make a foundation for the rock, two shifts of men were set at this work. In twenty days and nights, they constructed, with baling-wire, steel cable and two thousand cords of brush, about 13,000 square feet of mattress, which was enough to cover the bed of the river from shore to shore with a double thickness of blanketing about one hundred feet in width. When this covering had been completed and sunk, a railway trestle ten feet wide was built across the crevasse, and on the 14th of September work-trains of "battleships" began running across it and dumping rock on to the mattress at the bottom of the stream. Meanwhile, the by-pass to the Rockwood head-gate was completed and enlarged, and in less than two weeks the dam was high enough to close the crevasse in part and thus divert water through the by-pass and gate. On the 10th of October, nearly 13,000 cubic feet of water per second was passing through the gate, while only one-tenth of that amount was flowing over the dam. The gate, however, under the pressure to which it was subjected, both by the water and by great masses of accumulated driftwood, began to show signs of weakness, and at two o'clock on the following day two-thirds of it gave way, went out, and floated down stream. The by-pass then became the main river, while the top of the diversion dam was left practically dry. Thus ended, in almost complete failure, the fifth attempt to control the Colorado. The river had been barred in one channel, but it burst through another, carrying with it a 200-foot head-gate which represented four months of labor and an expenditure of $122,000.

Mr. Harriman and the Southern Pacific engineers were disappointed but not disheartened. The steel-and-concrete head-gate at Andrade had been ready for use since June, and powerful dredges were set at work clearing out and enlarging the four miles of silted-up canal south of it, so that water might be furnished to the Imperial Valley by that route while another attempt was being made to close completely both the Rockwood by-pass and the original intake.

An inspection of the rock-fill dam, which had been left exposed by the diversion of the river, showed that the objections made to a structure of this kind were not well founded. The brush-mattress had not been broken by the weight of the rocks; the rocks themselves had not sunk out of sight in the soft silt of the bottom, and the dam had not been breached or seriously injured. It leaked a little, but its good condition in other respects suggested the possibility of quickly closing the by-pass and the intake with rock barriers of this type. Additional trestles were built across both waterways; ten trains of flat cars and "battleships" were set at work bringing rock from three or four different quarries, and the laboring force was increased to about a thousand men with seven hundred horses and mules. Operations were pushed night and day, and in a little more than three weeks, high rock-fill dams were built across both intake and by-pass, and were connected by massive levees so as to make a continuous barrier about half a mile in length. Leakage through the dams was stopped by facing them with gravel and clay, forced into the interstices and puddled with streams of water from powerful pumps, and the levees at both ends were connected with those that had previously been built up and down the river by the California Development Company. In the course of the work there were used, first and last, about three thousand carloads of rock, gravel and clay, while 400,000 cubic yards of earth were moved by dredges and teams.

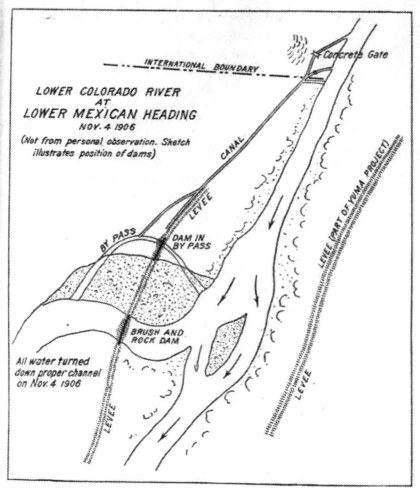

First Closure of Crevasse, Nov. 4, 1906

THE SALTON SEA

On the 4th of November, a little more than two years after the cutting of the lower Mexican intake, the crevasse into which it had grown was closed, and the river was forced back into its ancient bed. The danger had apparently been averted and the Imperial Valley was safe; but where a treacherous river like the Colorado is concerned, danger is never over and safety can be secured only by incessant watchfulness and continual labor. On the 7th of December, another sudden flood came down the Gila and increased the discharge of the Colorado from 9000 to about 45,000 cubic feet per second. The rock-fill dam of the Southern Pacific engineers stood fast; but, about midnight, a reconstructed earthen levee of the California Development Company, twelve or fifteen hundred feet further south, was undermined, began to leak, and finally gave way. The breach at first was small; but it was so rapidly deepened and widened by erosion and caving that it soon became a crevasse, and in less than three days the whole river was pouring through a break a thousand feet wide and again rushing down the slope of the basin to the Salton Sea.

This new crevasse, taken in connection with the history and the experience of the two preceding years, showed conclusively: 1, that the

THE SALTON SEA

tendency of the Colorado to flow into the Salton Sink was increasing rather than diminishing; 2, that floods of from 180,000,000 to 360,000,000 cubic feet of water per hour were liable to occur at almost any season of the year; 3, that the defensive dikes of the California Development Company were everywhere inadequate or untrustworthy; and 4, that in order to afford certain protection to the Imperial Valley, it would be necessary not only to close the new break, but to build a stronger, higher and more massive levee along the west bank of the river for a distance of at least twenty miles.

These considerations raised of course the question whether it was worth while for the Southern Pacific Company to continue this work, upon which it had already spent about $1,500,000. The interests chiefly imperilled were those of the national Government. It owned all the irrigable land along the lower Colorado, including even that upon which the Imperial Valley settlers had filed.[1] It was then constructing an immense dam at Potholes,

---
[1] The settlers had made desert or homestead entries on the land, were actually in possession of it, and had an equitable right to it; but the original survey of this part of California had been found inaccurate and defective, and the Government would not—possibly could not—issue patents until boundaries had been more clearly defined by a re-survey. The settlers, therefore, could not raise money

twelve miles above Yuma, upon which it had already expended about $1,000,000 (the Laguna dam) and with the water to be impounded thereby it expected to irrigate and reclaim about 90,000 acres of fertile land in Arizona and Southern California. If the uncontrolled river should continue to "cut back," by means of its receding waterfalls, it not only would destroy the Laguna dam, and the irrigation works upon which the Imperial Valley depended for its very existence, but would eventually turn the whole bed of the lower Colorado into a gorge, out of which water for irrigation purposes could never be taken. This would make valueless more than two thousand square miles of potentially fertile land, which, if intensively cultivated, would support a quarter of a million people.

The interests of the Southern Pacific Company, on the other hand, were comparatively unimportant. The traffic of the Imperial Valley, at that time, amounted to perhaps $1,200,000 a year, from which the railroad derived a revenue of only $20,000 or $30,000 for freight transportation.[1] This, in its relation to

on their farms by mortgaging them, because the legal title was still vested in the Government. This became a very serious matter when they wished to help the Southern Pacific in its fight with the river.

[1] Maxwell Evarts.

THE SALTON SEA

the whole business of the company, was so insignificant as hardly to be worth consideration. The flooding of the valley, moreover, could not injure the road much more than it had already been injured. A section of new line, about sixty miles in length, had been surveyed and graded, and the ties and rails for it were on the ground. At an additional cost therefore of only $50,000 or $60,000, the imperilled part of the track could be moved to a higher location where the rising waters of the Salton Sea could not reach it.

President Randolph, after full investigation reported the existing state of affairs to Mr. Harriman by telegraph, and informed him that while the original break might be closed at a cost of from $300,000 to $350,000, permanent control of the river would require about twenty miles of muck-ditching [1] and levee reconstruction, and that if he (Mr. Harriman) decided to proceed with the work, he might have to spend $1,500,000, more. In view of this possibility, Mr. Randolph suggested that the Government, or the State of California, be called upon to render aid.

---

[1] Where the soil, on the site of a proposed levee, is loose and porous, so that water percolates rapidly through it, a "muck-ditch" is dug, to a depth of six or eight feet; material of more solid consistency is packed into it, and the levee is then built on the impervious foundation.

THE SALTON SEA

Mr. Harriman, who had implicit confidence in the sound business judgment as well as the engineering ability of Mr. Epes Randolph, accepted the latter's view of the situation. He did not doubt that the Colorado River might ultimately be controlled; but as the expense would be very great, and as the chief interests imperilled were those of the nation, he did not think that the Southern Pacific Company, of which he was President, was equitably or morally bound to do the work alone and at its own expense. In a long telegram to President Roosevelt, dated New York December 13th, he fully set forth the state of affairs, but did not comment upon it further than by saying: "In view of the above, it does not seem fair that we should be called to do more than join in to help the settlers."

The following telegraphic correspondence then ensued:

Washington, December 15, 1906.

MR. E. H. HARRIMAN,
   New York.

Referring to your telegram of December 13, I assume you are planning to continue work immediately on closing break in Colorado River. I should be fully informed as to how far you intend to proceed in the matter.

THEODORE ROOSEVELT.

THE SALTON SEA

New York, December 19, 1906.
THE PRESIDENT,
   Washington.

Further referring to your telegram of the 15th inst. our engineers advise that closing the break and restoring the levees can be most quickly and cheaply done, if the work is undertaken immediately, at a cost of $300,000 to $350,000. The Southern Pacific Company, having been at an expense of about $2,000,000 already, does not feel warranted in assuming this responsibility and the additional expenditure which is likely to follow to make the work permanent, besides the expenditure which the company is already undergoing to put its tracks above danger line. We are willing to coöperate with the Government, contributing train service, use of tracks and switches, use of rock quarries, train crews etc., and the California Development Company will contribute its engineers and organization, the whole work to be done under the Reclamation Service. Can you bring this about?

E. H. HARRIMAN.

Washington, December 20, 1906.
E. H. HARRIMAN,
   New York.

Replying to yours of 19th, Reclamation Service cannot enter upon work without authority of Congress and suitable convention with Mexico. Congress adjourns today for holidays. Impossible to secure action at present. It is

THE SALTON SEA

incumbent upon you to close break again. Question of future permanent maintenance can then be taken up. Reclamation engineers available for consultation. That is all the aid that there is in the power of the Government to render, and it seems to me clear that it is the imperative duty of the California Development Company to close this break at once.

The danger is ultimately due only to the action of that company in the past in making heading completed in October, 1904, in Mexican territory. The present crisis can at this moment only be met by the action of the company which is ultimately responsible for it, and that action should be taken without an hour's delay. Through the Department of State I am endeavoring to secure such action by the Mexican Government as will enable Congress in its turn to act. But at present Congress can do nothing without such action by the Mexican Government.

This is a matter of such vital importance that I wish to repeat that there is not the slightest excuse for the California Development Company waiting an hour for the action of the Government. It is its duty to meet the present danger immediately, and then this Government will take up with it, as it has already taken up with Mexico, the question of providing in permanent shape against the recurrence of the danger.

THEODORE ROOSEVELT.

Seldom, if ever before, in our country, had

material and financial interests of such tremendous importance been dependent upon the decision of a single man. If Mr. Harriman should order a continuance of the work, he would put at hazard a million and a half dollars of his own money, or the money of the Southern Pacific stockholders, in addition to the million and a half or two millions already spent. He would have to do this, moreover, mainly for the benefit of the Imperial Valley and the nation, without any assurance of reimbursement or compensation, and without any certainty of success. If, on the other hand, he should decline to sink any more capital in the effort to retrieve a disaster for which neither he nor the Southern Pacific Company was in the slightest degree responsible, the Laguna dam and the Imperial Valley would both be destroyed; twelve thousand ruined and impoverished people would be driven out into the desert, and 1,600,000 acres of Government land would be lost to the nation forever.

Mr. Harriman, at that time, was being prosecuted by the Interstate Commerce Commission as presumably a malefactor, and President Roosevelt, only a few weeks before, had characterized him as an "undesirable citizen;" but in the supreme test of character to which he was subjected, he showed magnanimity, courage and public spirit. On the same day that he received the President's telegram of December 20th, he replied in the following words:

"You seem to be under the impression that the California Development Company is a Southern Pacific enterprise. This is erroneous. It had nothing to do with its work, or the opening of the canal. We are not interested in its stock and in no way control it. We have loaned it some money to assist in dealing with the situation. What the Southern Pacific has done was for the protection of the settlers as well as of its own tracks, but we have determined to remove the tracks onto high ground anyway. However, in view of your message, I am giving authority to the Southern Pacific officers in the West to proceed at once with efforts to repair the break, trusting that the Government, as soon as you can procure the necessary Congressional action, will assist us with the burden."

The contention of the Government was that inasmuch as the Southern Pacific Company loaned $200,000 to the California Development Company in June, 1905, and assumed temporary control of the latter's affairs for the purpose of safeguarding its loan, the lending company thereby made itself responsible for all the unforeseen consequences of a ditch dug by the

THE SALTON SEA

borrowing company almost a year earlier. This contention will not bear a moment's scrutiny. The Southern Pacific Company did not, at any time, own any of the Development Company's stock. The shares pledged as collateral for the loan were in the hands of a trustee. The Southern Pacific Company did not even elect the president and three directors of the Development Company. They were elected by the latter's stockholders under the terms of the loan agreement.[1] The Southern Pacific was a creditor of the Development Company, but in no sense a "successor in interest" by virtue of ownership.

The lower Mexican intake, which admitted the river to the Valley and caused the disaster, was dug long before the Southern Pacific Company had any control whatever over the Development Company, and it would be a violation of the most elementary principles of equity if a lender were held responsible for all previous transactions of a borrower, merely because the latter had voluntarily agreed to share control of his business in order to obtain the loan. If a farmer goes to a bank, gives a mortgage on his

---

[1] The text of the agreement may be found in Report 1936, House of Representatives, 61st Congress, 3rd Session, Jan. 18, 1911.

farm as security for a loan, and agrees that a representative of the bank shall supervise his agricultural operations until the loan is repaid, the bank does not become responsible for a dam across a stream on the farmer's property built by the farmer himself a year before he had any relations with the bank. The bank might be responsible for a dam built under the direction of its representative, but not for a dam built by the farmer a year before such representative was appointed.

When President Roosevelt received Mr. Harriman's telegram of December 20th, saying that orders had been given to proceed with the work, he replied in the following words:

"Am delighted to receive your telegram. Have at once directed the Reclamation Service to get into touch with you, so that as soon as Congress reassembles I can recommend legislation which will provide against a repetition of the disaster and make provision for the equitable distribution of the burden."

While the negotiations between President Roosevelt and Mr. Harriman were in progress, the river-fighting organization on the lower Colorado was kept intact. The rock quarry at Andrade was further developed; sidings just

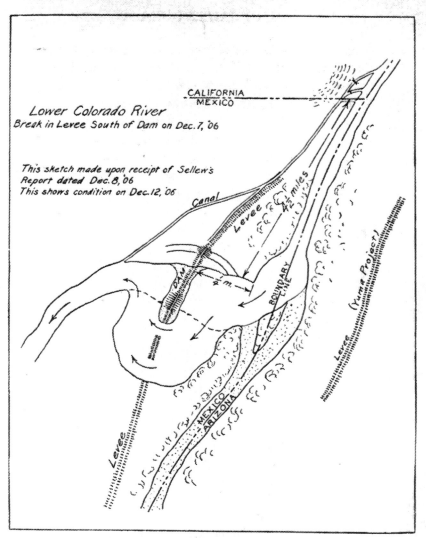

Last Break in Defences, December 1906

THE SALTON SEA

across the Mexican boundary were lengthened to seven thousand feet, and material and equipment of all possible kinds which might be needed were gathered and held in readiness. When, therefore, on the 20th of December, an order was received from Mr. Harriman to go ahead and close the break, President Randolph, backed by all the resources of the Southern Pacific, began a last supreme effort to control the river and save the Imperial Valley. The crevasse, at that time, was 1100 feet wide, with a maximum depth of forty feet, and the whole current of the Colorado was rushing through it and discharging into the basin of the Sink about 160,000,000 cubic feet of water every hour. There was not time enough for the construction of another brush-mattress, so the Southern Pacific engineers determined to build two railway trestles of ninety-foot piles across the break, and then, with a thousand flat cars and "battleships," bring rocks and dump them into the river faster than they could possibly be swallowed up by the silt or carried down stream. Three times, within a month, the ninety-foot piles were ripped out and swept away and the trestles partly or wholly destroyed; but the pile-drivers kept at work, and on the 27th of January the first trestle was

THE SALTON SEA

finished for the fourth time and the dumping of rock from it began.

Mr. F. H. Newell, Director of the U. S. Reclamation Service, in a description of the final closure of the crevasse, says:

"The stones used were as large as could be handled or pushed from the flat cars by a gang of men, or by as many men as could get around a stone. In some cases the pieces were so large that it was necessary to break them by what are called 'pop-shots' of dynamite laid upon the stone while it rested on the cars. In this way the stones were broken and then could be readily thrown overboard by hand. The scene at the closure of the break was exciting. Train after train with heavy locomotives came to the place and the stones, large and small, were pushed off by hundreds of workmen as rapidly as the cars could be placed. While waiting to get out upon the trestle the larger stones were broken by 'pop-shots,' and the noise sounded like artillery in action. Added to the roar of the waters were the whistle signals, the orders to the men, and the bustle of an army working day and night to keep ahead of the rapid cutting of the stream.

"As the rock heap rose gradually, it checked the river, causing it also to rise higher and

THE SALTON SEA

higher and to cascade over the pile of stone. Riffles were caused, and an undercutting of the lower slope of the rock heap allowed it to settle and the stones to roll down stream. All of this undercutting and settling had to be made up and overcome by the rapid dumping of other large stones."

"It was necessary to raise the river bodily about eleven feet. As the water rose and became ponded on the upper side of the rock heap, train load after train load of small stone and gravel from the nearby hills was dumped to fill the spaces between the large rocks. Finally, after days and nights of struggle, the water was raised to a point where it began to flow down its former channel and less and less to pass over the rock heap. Then finer material was added and rapidly piled up on the accumulated rock mass. At first, a large amount of water passed through, and steps were taken as rapidly as possible to close the openings by dumping sand and gravel, finishing this work by hydraulicking silt or mud over the area and washing this in with a hose. By thus piling up finer and finer material and distributing it, the seepage or percolation through the mass was quickly checked and the barrier became effective." ("The Salton Sea," by F. H. Newell,

THE SALTON SEA

Director of the U. S. Reclamation Service; Annual Report of the Smithsonian Institution for 1907, p. 331.)

The crevasse was closed and the river forced into its old bed on the 10th of February 1907, fifty two days after President Roosevelt appealed to Mr. Harriman, and fifteen days after the first "battleship" load of rock was dumped from the first completed trestle. In order, however, that this gigantic work might be accomplished, the transportation of commercial freight on the western part of the transcontinental railroad had to be temporarily abandoned. In testifying before a House committee, about a year later, Chief Engineer Cory said:

"For three weeks, two divisions of the Southern Pacific system, embracing about twelve hundred miles of main line, were practically tied up because of our demands for equipment and facilities. We had a thousand flat cars exclusively in our service, and shipping from Los Angeles' seaport—San Pedro—was practically abandoned for two weeks until we returned a considerable portion of the equipment. It was simply a case of putting rock into that break faster than the river could take it away. . . . In fifteen days after we got the trestle across and dumped the first carload of rock we had the river stopped. In that time I suppose we handled rock faster than it was ever handled before. . . . We hauled it from Patagonia, Arizona, four hundred and eighty five miles, over two mountain passes; from Tacna, sixty miles to the east; from three other quarries—one on the Santa Fé, one on the Salt Lake road, and one on the Southern Pacific—all near Colton, two hundred miles to the west, and over the San Gorgonio Pass. . . . We brought in about three thousand flat cars loaded with rock from these immense distances, and we put in, all together, about 80,000 cubic yards of rock in fifteen days."

But the work of the Southern Pacific engineers was not confined solely to the closing of the crevasse. In order to prevent a future break in some other part of the irrigation company's defensive system, they were compelled to extend their branch railway, and to build or reinforce levees all up and down the river. Describing this work soon after its completion in 1907, the Director of the U. S. Reclamation Service said:

"There now extends from the head works in the United States along the river, between it and the canal, a double row of dikes, the outer

Hind-Clarke Dam by which Crevasse was Finally Closed in January 1907

Railroad Track on Reconstructed Levee

THE SALTON SEA

one being occupied by a railroad. These extend in an unbroken line for a dozen miles near the river and shut it off from the lowlands to the west. The river side of this dike is protected by a thick layer of gravel, and the railroad affords immediate access to all parts, so that if menaced by the cutting of the banks it will be possible to bring men and materials to check the floods from encroachment upon the dike itself. Secondary dikes or cross levees run from the main structure to certain subsidiary works, so that if the outer main dike is broken or water flows through, this will be ponded, for a while at least, against the inner line of defense, thus affording time to assemble the necessary equipment to fight another intrusion."

In closing the second crevasse and completing the so-called "Hind-Clarke dam [1] there were used 1200 ninety-foot piles; 16,000 feet of eight-by-seventeen-inch pine stringers, and 5765 carloads of rock, gravel and clay. In reconstructing and extending the levee system nearly 900,000 cubic yards of earth were excavated or placed in embankments, while 5285 carloads of

[1] The northern part of this dam, across the by-pass and intake, was built under the immediate supervision of Superintendent Thomas J. Hind, and the southern part, across the second crevasse, under that of Superintendent C. K. Clarke. Both were Southern Pacific engineers.

gravel for blanketing were brought from the Mammoth Gravel Pit, forty miles west of the river on the main line. The total cost of the defensive work done after President Roosevelt made his appeal to Mr. Harriman was about $1,600,000, and this added to the cost of previous operations made a total of approximately $3,100,000 expended in the effort to control the Colorado and keep it out of the Imperial Valley. But the work was thoroughly and effectively done. The river has never broken through the Southern Pacific defences, although since the final closing of the second crevasse in 1907 there have been two floods in which the discharge of water has exceeded 140,000 cubic feet per second, or twelve billion cubic feet every twenty four hours.

The great service thus rendered by Mr. Harriman to the people of the Imperial Valley and to the nation has never been set forth more clearly, perhaps, than it was in the message sent by President Roosevelt to the Congress on the 12th of January 1907, while the work of closing the second crevasse was in progress. In that historic paper he said:

"The governor of the State of California and individuals and communities in southern California have made urgent appeals to me to take

THE SALTON SEA

steps to save the lands and settlements in the sink, or depression, known as the Imperial Valley, or Salton Sink region, from threatened destruction by the overflow of Colorado River. The situation appears so serious and urgent that I now refer the matter to the Congress for its consideration. . . .

"By means of the facilities available to the Southern Pacific Company, the break in the west bank of the Colorado River was closed on November 4, 1906. A month later, however, a sudden rise in the river undermined the poorly constructed levees immediately south of the former break, and the water again resumed its course into the Salton Sea.

"The results have been highly alarming, as it appears that if the water is not checked it will cut a very deep channel which, progressing upstream in a series of cataracts, will result in conditions such that the water cannot be diverted by gravity into the canals already built in the Imperial Valley. If the break is not closed before the coming spring flood of 1907, it appears highly probable that all of the property values created in this valley will be wiped out, including farms and towns, as well as the revenues derived by the Southern Pacific Company. Ultimately the channel will be deepened in the main stream itself, up to and beyond the town of Yuma, destroying the homes and farms there, the great railroad bridge, and the Government works at Laguna dam above Yuma. . . .

"If the river is not put back and permanently maintained in its natural bed, the progressive back-cutting, in the course of one or two years, will extend upstream to Yuma, as before stated, and finally to the Laguna dam, now being built by the Government, thus wiping out millions of dollars of property belonging to the Government and to citizens. Continuing farther, it will deprive all the valley lands along the Colorado River of the possibility of obtaining necessary supply of water by gravity canals.

"The great Yuma bridge will go out, and approximately 700,000 acres of land as fertile as the Nile Valley will be left in a desert condition. What this means may be understood when we remember that the entire producing area of southern California is about 250,000 acres. A most conservative estimate after full development must place the gross product from this land at not less than $100 per acre per year, every ten acres of which will support a family when under intense cultivation. If the break in the Colorado is not permanently controlled,

THE SALTON SEA

the financial loss to the United States will be great. The entire irrigable area which will be either submerged or deprived of water, in the Imperial Valley and along the Colorado River, is capable of adding to the permanent population of Arizona and California at least 350,000 people, and probably 500,000. Much of the land will be worth from $500 to $1500 per acre to individual owners, or a total of from $350,000,000 to $700,000,000. . . .

"The point to be especially emphasized is that prompt action must be taken, if any; otherwise the conditions may become so extreme as to be impracticable of remedy. . . . It is probable now that with an expenditure of $2,000,000 the river can be restored to its former channel and held there indefinitely; but if this action is not taken immediately, several times this sum may be required to restore it, and possibly it cannot be restored unless enormous sums are expended." (House Report No. 1936, 61st Congress, 3rd Session, pp. 153-157.)

The Recompense

One might naturally suppose that when a private citizen, at the head of a great railroad company, averted a national calamity, and saved for the country public property that was actually worth $25,000,000 and that had a potential value of "from $350,000,000 to $700,000,000," he would be entitled, at least, to the thanks of the national legislature. If, even in Russia, a railroad president, at the request of the Czar, controlled a great flood in the Volga, barred that river out of the city of Astrakhan, and saved from total destruction "700,000 acres" of fertile land potentially worth "from $350,000,000 to $700,000,000," he would certainly receive the thanks of the nation, expressed in a suitably worded resolution of the Duma and the Council of the Empire. It is more than probable that, even in China, something of this kind would have been done for a railroad president who had controlled a disastrous flood in the valley of the Hoang-ho. But no such acknowledgment of valuable service was ever made by the Congress of the United States.

Perhaps, however, Mr. Harriman was not entitled to credit, for the reason that the work in the field was done by the Southern Pacific Company and its engineers. This was not the view taken by the company and the engineers themselves. If Mr. Harriman, personally, had been asked who finally controlled the Colorado

THE SALTON SEA

River and saved the Imperial Valley, he undoubtedly would have replied: "Epes Randolph, H. T. Cory, Thomas J. Hind, C. K. Clarke, and their associates." But these gentlemen have publicly said that the driving power behind their work—the one thing that made it successful—was the invincible determination of their chief. In a written discussion of the operations on the lower Colorado, which was conducted by the American Society of Civil Engineers, Mr. C. K. Clarke said:

"The writer desires to put on record the fact that the accomplishment of the work was due primarily and exclusively to the independent judgment and courage of Mr. Harriman, who persisted in his belief that the breaks could be closed, and his determination to close them, in the face of opposition, and regardless of the positive assertions of a host of eminent engineers that the closure was a physical impossibility." (Transactions of the American Society of Civil Engineers, Paper 1270, pp. 1551–2.)

In the course of the same discussion, Mr. Elwood Mead, Chief of the Irrigation and Drainage Division of the U. S. Department of Agriculture, said:

"It was the duty of the State or Nation to take charge, and provide the money and men needed to restore the river to its former channel. Apparently no one in authority was interested; the State Government only considered the matter long enough to write a letter to the President, and the President, having Congress on his hands, shifted the responsibility to the head of a railroad company; and it was not until the railroad company took charge that we have the first refreshing example of generosity and public spirit. Nothing could have been finer than the action of Mr. Harriman. The loan of $250,000, when his time and resources were overtaxed by the earthquake at San Francisco, and the providing more than $1,000,000 for the last hazardous attempt to save the valley, furnish an inspiring contrast to the supine indifference and irresponsibility shown by both the State and Federal authorities." (Same Paper, p. 1510.)

Mr. Epes Randolph, who as President of the California Development Company directed and controlled the engineering operations in the lower Colorado from 1905 to 1907, said, in a private letter to a student of the subject:

"It was a great work, and I do not believe that any man whom I have ever known, except Mr. Harriman, would have undertaken it. All of those of us who actually handled the work

THE SALTON SEA

were merely instruments in the hands of the Master Builder."

From these expressions of opinion it clearly appears that, in the judgment of the men "on the firing line," the fight with the Colorado was inspired, directed and won by E. H. Harriman; but no acknowledgment of indebtedness to him personally was ever made by the Congress of the United States. The service that he personally rendered was recognized and publicly acknowledged only by the people of the Imperial Valley. In testifying before the House Claims Committee, in March 1910, Mr. J. B. Parazette, speaking for the farmers of the Valley, said:

"We do feel rather differently in that Valley toward Mr. Harriman from the way others seem to feel elsewhere over the United States. We believe that Mr. Harriman felt a very human interest in our troubles there. . . . We volunteered to furnish about five hundred horses, and to bed and board them, and to furnish men to work during the time that the break was being closed; but we heard that Mr. Harriman said that the farmers down there, he supposed, had a great deal to do (it was seeding time with them) and they had about all the work to attend to that they could handle, and the Southern Pacific would fix the break anyway. What we could have done would not have amounted to much to the railroad company, but it would have amounted to considerable to the farmers there, taking their teams out at that time of the year when they wanted to put in crops."

This expression of gratitude to Mr. Harriman for "showing a human interest" in the farmers' "troubles," and for declining to increase their hardships by shifting a part of the burden of work from his own shoulders to theirs, must have pleased him more than any formal vote of thanks from Congress could have done.

When Mr. Harriman, on the 20th of December 1906, telegraphed the President that, "in view of" his "message," he would resume efforts to control the Colorado, he ventured to express the modest hope that the Government, as soon as the necessary Congressional action could be secured, would "assist with the burden." Mr. Roosevelt replied that he would recommend legislation to "provide against a repetition of the disaster and make provision for an equitable distribution of the burden." (House Report No. 1936, 61st Congress, 3rd Session, p. 163). Three weeks later, however, when the work was actually in progress, he merely said, in his message to Congress, that "the question as to what sum, *if any*, should

THE SALTON SEA

be paid to the Southern Pacific Company for work done since the break of November 4th, 1906, is one for future consideration. For work done prior to that date no claim can be admitted" (Same Report, p. 157). This may have seemed to Mr. Roosevelt a proper recommendation, and one likely to secure "an equitable distribution of the burden;" but it would not have made that impression upon an irrigation expert, say, from the planet Mars, because it suggested a doubt whether "*any*" of the burden should be borne by the chief beneficiary, namely the Government. However, when a bill to reimburse the Southern Pacific Company was introduced in the House of Representatives in 1908, the President did give it cordial support by saying, in a letter to the chairman of the Claims Committee:

". . . I accordingly wrote an earnest appeal to the officials of the road" (the Southern Pacific) "asking them to act. They did act, and thereby saved from ruin many people in southern California, and saved to the Government the Laguna dam. . . . I feel that it is an act of justice to act generously in this matter, for the railroad, by the prompt and effective work that it did, rendered a notable service to the threatened community. In no other way could this result have been accomplished."

THE SALTON SEA

(House Report No. 1936, 61st Congress, 3rd Session.)

Mr. Roosevelt's "earnest appeal" had been addressed, as a matter of fact, to E. H. Harriman, not to "the officials of the road;" but the President, apparently, could not bring himself, either in this letter or in his previous message, to mention the name of the man who, at the very time when he was struggling with the Colorado River at the request of the Government, was being prosecuted by that same Government as a malefactor. Names are often embarrassing, and the name in this case might have suggested to the public mind the obnoxious idea that Mr. Harriman, after all, might not be a wholly "undesirable citizen." Then, too, there would have been a certain incongruity in denouncing "Harriman," by name as a public enemy, while asking the same "Harriman," by name, to render a great public service; so it was apparently thought safer to mention the name in one case and drop it out of sight in the other.

The President's appeal to Congress to "act generously," was not so successful as had been his appeal to Mr. Harriman to stop the Colorado River and save the Imperial Valley. Congress seldom acts "generously" except on measures likely to influence votes, such as pension bills,

THE SALTON SEA

public building bills, and bills for the improvement of rivers and harbors. Mr. Harriman and the Southern Pacific Company had "improved" a national river, at a cost to themselves of about $3,000,000; but inasmuch as they were then under a cloud of unpopularity created by official and unofficial misrepresentation, their influence on Congressional elections was negligible, and Senators and Representatives might safely—perhaps judiciously—ignore their claim regardless of its merits. The reimbursement bill, therefore, dragged along without action for about three years. Hearings were held, witnesses from California and Arizona were examined, expert engineers were consulted, and the whole subject was thoroughly threshed out. Memorials in support of the bill were received from towns, communities and chambers of commerce in the Imperial Valley; and the entire Congressional delegation from California, as well as almost all the newspapers of the State, urged reimbursement as a matter of simple justice. But Congress could not make up its mind to do justice, either to Mr. Harriman or to a railroad company. In 1909, when William H. Taft became President, he at once took up the matter, and in his first message to Congress referred to it in the following words:

THE SALTON SEA

"This leads me to invite the attention of Congress to the claim made by the Southern Pacific Company for an amount expended in a similar work of relief called for by a flood and great emergency. This work, as I am informed, was undertaken at the request of my predecessor, and under promise to reimburse the railroad company. It seems to me the equity of this claim is manifest, and the only question involved is the reasonable value of the work done. I recommend the payment of the claim, in a sum found to be just." (House Report No. 1956, 61st Congress, 3rd Session.)

Two years later, when nothing had been done, President Taft sent to the Chairman of the House Committee on Claims the following letter:

White House
Washington, Jan. 16, 1911.
HON. GEORGE W. PRINCE,
Chairman of Committee on Claims,
My dear Mr. Prince:
As I recommended in my message, I sincerely hope that Congress, at this time, will compensate the Southern Pacific Railway for work which it did in the Imperial Valley under stress of great emergency. I do not know what amount is just, but I do know that that company came to the rescue of the Government at the instance of President Roosevelt, and that there was an implied arrangement under which

THE SALTON SEA

they were to be compensated, and I think that Congress should take up the matter and do justice to that corporation in this instance.

Sincerely yours,
W. H. TAFT.

Under this pressure from the White House, the Committee on Claims finally acted. On the 28th of January 1911, after having reduced the proposed appropriation from $1,663,000 to $773,000, the committee, by a divided vote, reported the bill to the House with the recommendation that it pass. Five members, however, namely Representatives Goldfogle, Kitchin, Candler, Shackleford and Adair, presented a minority report in which they described the bill as "an attempted raid on the Federal Treasury;" denied that there was "any legal, equitable, or moral obligation on the part of the Government" to pay this sum, "or any amount, for closing the break in the Colorado River;" referred to the proposed appropriation as "purely a gratuity," "a gift of the people's money," and declared that they were opposed to this "gift to the Southern Pacific Company, as well as all other gratuities to private enterprise." (House Report No. 1936, part 2; 61st Congress, 3rd Session.)

This minority report seems to have given

the *coup de grace* to the reimbursement bill. Whether the members of the House were lacking in a sense of justice; whether they were indifferent to the bill because there was "nothing in it for them;" or whether they were afraid, in an election campaign, to face the charge that they had "given the people's money," as "a pure gratuity" to one of Mr. Harriman's railroad corporations, it is impossible to say. Certain it is that no action was ever taken on the bill, although it had been favorably reported by the Committee on Claims; had been repeatedly recommended by two Presidents, and had been unanimously supported, regardless of party lines, by the people of the Imperial Valley and by the whole State of California. There are certain events which may seem inexplicable, but upon which it is not necessary to comment. The barest recital of facts is eloquent enough.

Shortly before his death, Mr. Harriman made a trip through the Imperial Valley and over the reconstructed levee which kept the Colorado River within bounds. Upon his return to Imperial Junction, he was met by a representative of the Los Angeles Examiner who, in conversation about the work, said:

"Mr. Harriman, the Government hasn't paid you that money, and your work here does not

THE SALTON SEA

seem to be duly appreciated; do you not, under the circumstances, regret having made this large expenditure?"

"No," replied Mr. Harriman. "This valley was worth saving, wasn't it?"

"Yes," said the reporter.

"Then we have the satisfaction of knowing that we saved it, haven't we?"

It is unfortunate that so fine an achievement as the controlling of the Colorado River and the saving of the Imperial Valley should have been clouded by national ingratitude or indifference; but if Mr. Harriman were living today, he would doubtless find compensation and satisfaction enough in the results of his work as they now appear. The Salton Sea, which once threatened to submerge and destroy the artificially created oasis in the desert, ceased to rise in 1907 and is now slowly drying up. The great Laguna dam above Yuma is done, and is furnishing water to tens of thousands of acres in southern California and Arizona. The territory along the Colorado River below the Grand Cañon, whose prospective value President Roosevelt estimated at "from $350,000,000 to $700,000,000" is safe. The Imperial Valley, which was yielding only $1,200,000 to its cultivators ten years ago, is now producing cotton,

THE SALTON SEA

barley, alfalfa, cantaloupes, grapes, vegetables and live stock worth more than ten times that amount. According to an estimate made by the Imperial Valley Press in June, 1916, the farmers of the Valley will earn this year a sum equivalent to the interest on $500,000,000. And all of this actual and potential wealth, as well as the land that has produced or will produce it, was threatened with total destruction in 1906, and was saved for the nation by the constructive genius and the invincible resolution of the "Master Builder."

Printed in the United States of America

THE following pages contain advertisements of a few of the Macmillan books on kindred subjects.

Italy, France and Britain at War

By H. G. WELLS,
Author of "Mr. Britling Sees it Through," "What is Coming," etc.

Cloth, 12mo. $1.50

Mr. Wells first discusses the changing sentiment as regards the war in the different countries where it is being waged. He then takes up the war in Italy—The Isonzo Front, The Mountain Warfare, and Behind the Front. After this comes a section devoted to the Western war, with chapters on Ruins, Grades of War, The War Landscape, New Arms for Old Ones, and Tanks. Finally comes the part in which Mr. Wells asks, "What do people think about the war?" Here he presents such problems as "Do they really think at all?, The Yielding Pacifist, and The Conscientious Objector, The Religious Revival, The Riddle of the British, The Social Changes in Progress and The Ending of the War."

The dates appended to the different chapters show that they were written the latter part of 1916, thus embodying the distinguished author's latest thoughts on the European tragedy.

"Rarely has Mr. Wells sent forth a volume more brilliant, keener in its thinking, truer in its perceptions, while the author's restless intelligence makes it possible, necessary indeed, for him to include such questions as the world control of agriculture, the development of a new religion, the passing of the hero, the other matters upon which he talks with illumination and the deepest conviction. . . . He has said it with compactness and earnestness and in neat, closely trimmed sentences that often sparkle with epigrammatic wit."—*N. Y. Times.*

"Mr. Wells, the pacifist, has contributed to the literature of the war the most brilliant exposition yet published. There are many great pages in the volume—those on the effigy and General Joffre and the perfected French method of offensive warfare, for instance; and his comparison between the French and English officers is a miracle of frankness. . . .—*Philadelphia Public Ledger.*

THE MACMILLAN COMPANY
Publishers   64-66 Fifth Avenue   New York

American World Policies

By WALTER E. WEYL,
Author of "The New Democracy"

Cloth, $2.25

Walter E. Weyl will be remembered as the author of *The New Democracy*, one of the most significant books dealing with the spirit of American life. Dr. Weyl is not a prolific writer—in consequence everything that he publishes is well considered; the product of prolonged investigation and study. A new work of his, entitled *American World Policies*, promises to have a wide appeal.

The United States is deeply concerned with the peace that is to come at the end of the war, and with the great society that is to be reconstituted then. The fact that America's position in the international situation has been complicated within the last few weeks increases this interest and makes the publication of Dr. Weyl's book most timely. For *American World Policies* seeks, on the basis of economic research, to define this country's attitude towards Expansion, Imperialism, the Establishment of International Government and more particularly its proper relations to the Monroe Doctrine, Mexico, China, Japan, the British Empire, the little and big nations of Europe and the rule of the sea. The book relates our foreign policies to our internal problems, to the clash of industrial classes and of political parties, to the decay of sectionalism and the slow growth of the national sense. It is a study of "Americanism" from without and within.

Dr. Weyl divides his twenty-one chapters into three parts. The first is entitled Our Idealistic Past, taking up such topics as Peace Without Effort, America Among the Nations, and The Unripe Imperialism. The second is The Root of Imperialism, and here are considered among other things The Integration of the World, Imperialism and War, The Revolt Against Imperialism, and The American Decision. The third section, Towards Economic Internationalism, considers An Antidote to Imperialism, American Interests Abroad, Pacifism, Static and Dynamic, Towards International Government, and The Forces of Internationalism. The work concludes with a chapter captioned The Immediate Program.

THE MACMILLAN COMPANY
Publishers   64–66 Fifth Avenue   New York

Brazil: Today and Tomorrow
By L. E. ELLIOTT

With Illustrations and Maps; decorated cloth, 12mo. $2.25

This volume seeks to show how and to what extent Brazil has been "opened up" and developed and by whom, and to outline some of the work that remains to be done. Miss Elliott first of all discusses present social conditions in Brazil, explaining who the Brazilian is, what political and social events have moulded him and what he has done to develop his territory; a territory 300,000 square miles larger than that of the United States. Later sections deal with finance, the monetary conditions of the country, the problem of exchange, and the source of income. Still others take up various means of transit, the railroads, the coastwise and the ocean service, rivers and roads. Industries are treated in considerable detail — cattle, cotton raising, weaving, coffee growing and the rubber trade.

The Danish West Indies
By WALDEMAR WESTERGAARD

With Maps and Illustrations

This volume presents for the first time a detailed and authoritative picture of Danish colonization in tropical America. It covers the administration of the Danish West India and Guinea Company (1671–1754), emphasizing the economic side, but touching on exploits of buccaneers and pirates, even Kidd himself. The work is based on extended research in Danish archives. It brings into clear relief that curious triangular commerce on the Atlantic typical of seventeenth and eighteenth century Europe.

Russia in 1916
By STEPHEN GRAHAM

$1.25

Mr. Graham continues to write books about Russia because he continues to visit that country and to see wholly interesting and unusual aspects of life there. This volume records his impressions during a tramping trip made in the summer of 1916. It embodies, then, his very latest ideas as to Russia and its people.

THE MACMILLAN COMPANY
Publishers   64-66 Fifth Avenue   New York

Alaska: The Great Country

BY ELLA HIGGINSON

New edition. With illustrations. Cloth, 8vo.

This remarkable volume first published in 1908 and since that time held to be as adequate a description of Alaska, its history, its scenery, its people, and its customs as has ever been written, now appears in a new edition with new matter. These added chapters have to do largely with the latest information about the railroads, the government, mining, fishing, merchandise shipments from Alaska and the agricultural development of the land.

Mount Rainier: A Record of Explorations

EDITED BY EDMOND S. MEANY,

Professor of History in the University of Washington, Author of "Vancouver's Discovery of Puget Sound," etc.

With illustrations. Cloth, 8vo. $2.50

This book seeks to give information about the discovery and exploration of Mt. Rainier and its environs. The discovery and naming of the mountain, the first recorded trip through Naches Pass in 1841, the first attempted ascent, and the first successful ascent, the explorations of the northern slopes, McClure's achievement and tragic death in 1897, the rocks, the glaciers and the flora—it is such topics as these that are considered. The volume is one of great interest and value to every lover of adventure or student of history.

THE MACMILLAN COMPANY
Publishers   64-66 Fifth Avenue   New York

PANAMA, the Canal, the Country, and the People

By ARTHUR BULLARD

Illustrated, new edition, 8°, $2.25

"A thoroughly satisfactory book for one who is looking for solid information." — *Boston Globe*.

"A most interesting picture of the country as it is to-day." — *San Francisco Chronicle*.

"One of the very few books on any Latin-American country that gives any idea of the whole land and people." — *Los Angeles Times*.

"One of the very best of travel books." — *Continent*.

"Lively and readable, containing the real atmosphere of the tropics." — *Minneapolis Tribune*.

"A book which every American ought to read, both for pleasure and profit." — *New York Herald*.

THE MACMILLAN COMPANY
Publishers   64–66 Fifth Avenue   New York

LaVergne, TN USA
12 October 2009
160628LV00006B/172/A